DISCARD

CHICAGO:
A
HISTORICAL GUIDE
TO THE
NEIGHBORHOODS
THE LOOP AND SOUTH SIDE

D1211550

View northeast across State and Madison, ca. 1906. This view and the signpost on the cover provide an appropriate beginning for this volume: the corner of State and Madison is the focal point for Chicago's oldest neighborhood and the changing character of the Loop's commercial activity has been one of the most influential factors in the development of other South Side neighborhoods. Cover photo by Paul W. Petraitis; frontispiece photo gift of Rand McNally & Co., CHS.

The maps which introduce the various neighborhoods in this book are portions of the 1909 edition of *The Rand-McNally New Standard Map of Chicago* updated through 1911. This base map was chosen because it antedates the numerous dramatic shifts in neighborhood boundaries and land available for housing and business brought about by modern urban renewal and highway construction. Map gift of Rand McNally & Co., CHS.

CHICAGO: A HISTORICAL GUIDE TO THE NEIGHBORHOODS

THE LOOP AND SOUTH SIDE

GLEN E. HOLT and DOMINIC A. PACYGA

CHICAGO HISTORICAL SOCIETY

1979

Publication of this volume
was made possible by support from
the Continental Bank Foundation

© 1979 by the Chicago Historical Society
All rights reserved

Library of Congress Card Catalog Number: 78—060184
ISBN: 0—913820—07—5

Editor: Fannia Weingartner
Designer: Herbert Slobin

CONTENTS

PREFACE

Chicago's neighborhoods are much in the news today. To some they represent the last bastions of ethnic or racial identity in an increasingly homogeneous society; to others they are barriers to the development of a larger and less parochial spirit in the city.

This guide to some of Chicago's historic neighborhoods of the South Side is the first of what we hope will be an important series interpreting the historical processes that have formed and shaped the city's community life. Both words and images have been used to create a historical and social iconography of each of the areas covered, in the hope that this combination will not only convey the changes that have occurred in each neighborhood, but will also impart a sense of each community's uniqueness.

In preparing this guide, its authors have remained keenly aware of their role as historians rather than as agents of community change. The history of the neighborhoods considered in this volume is not always pleasant. For some it is a story of stability and continuity; for others, a catalog of disintegration and decay; for others still, an affirmation of individual and group courage. What these neighborhoods have always had in common and still share today is a vitality that springs from the spirit of those who live there.

HAROLD K. SKRAMSTAD, JR.
DIRECTOR

ACKNOWLEDGMENTS

This book originated in a series of neighborhood tours which the authors conducted over the course of a year, beginning in the spring of 1976. The tours covered a triangular area extending from the Loop south to Hyde Park and west to Gage Park, and centered on the Union Stock Yards, Packingtown, and the Central Manufacturing District. In mid-1977, Professor Richard Jensen of the University of Illinois at Chicago Circle and Dr. Mark Friedberger, research associate in the Family and Community History Center of the Newberry Library (which sponsored the tours) encouraged us to write up our tour notes for use by participants in the local history workshops. With encouragement from Dr. Harold K. Skramstad, Jr., director of the Chicago Historical Society, and Dr. Richard Brown, director of research and education at the Newberry Library, we undertook the writing assignment.

As we set about our task we realized that there was a need that would not be met by our merely reproducing our tour narration in written form. Except for a few brief paragraphs of history for each of Chicago's seventy-five community areas in the various local community fact books—the last of which appeared after the census of 1960— little comparative historical study has been done on the city's neighborhoods. We therefore decided to write brief histories for one coherent group of communities on Chicago's South Side. The result is this guide.

Writing this book proved difficult. The overriding problem was to find adequate source material on several of the neighborhoods. Countless interested citizens and several scholars helped, taking the time to answer specific questions. While all of these people have our gratitude, three deserve special thanks: Ellen Skerrett drew on her own vast research on parish life to furnish us with information and photographs; Joseph Topor of the Polish Highlanders of America gave us access to his photo albums; and the Reverend Angelo U. Garbin, pastor of All Saints–St. Anthony of Padua parish, provided crucial information about several Catholic church movements. Without such assistance we would not have been able to write a history of several of the neighborhoods. As it is, a lack of information eventually prevented us from constructing even a simple narrative for Fuller Park, which is within our study area.

Once we had completed the basic manuscript, Grant Dean, reference librarian at the Chicago Historical Society, and the Reverend Andrew M. Greeley, well-known scholar of the city's neighborhoods, reviewed the manuscript for us.

Our debt does not end there, however. Fannia Weingartner, the Society's editor of publications, has labored long hours over this manuscript, helping us to set the tone of the work. Gail Casterline and Marcia Beales of the publications office also suggested changes. Julia Westerberg, assistant curator of graphics, and Mary Francis Rhymer, curator emeritus of graphics, not only located the photographs that we requested but turned up several we had not seen before. Walter W. Krutz and Paul W. Petraitis, staff photographers, also did more than was asked, using their technical skills to liven up marginal pieces and suggesting a number of photographs for inclusion. Herb Slobin provided the design which brings text and graphics together.

The National Endowment for the Humanities funded the Local History Project and the tours from which this book developed. Financial support from the Continental Bank Foundation made its publication possible.

GLEN E. HOLT and DOMINIC A. PACYGA

INTRODUCTION

In this volume the word "neighborhood" is used interchangeably with the word "community" and the phrase "community area." This usage follows the prevailing custom of those who live in the city's neighborhoods and is in accord with the tradition set by the Chicago School of Sociology during the 1920s. Led by Robert E. Park and Ernest W. Burgess, this group of scholars and their students set out to examine the complexities of the city's community life. As part of this study, they broke the city into "community areas" and to delimit these areas they first located "natural boundaries"—railroad lines and waterways which split the flat Chicago plain into myriad shapes. Where no such natural boundaries existed, the sociologists surveyed residents and examined traffic patterns and institutional use to locate the dividing lines among the functioning community areas. In only one case have we broken with a broad community area definition: within the New City community area, residents over the years have behaved as if there were at least two neighborhoods, Back of the Yards and Canaryville, and we have accordingly treated them separately.

Fundamentally, this book is concerned with the local manifestation of a demographic movement that is a national and, indeed, a world-wide phenomenon: the dispersal of population away from the center of cities. In Chicago, the point of origin for this movement has been the Loop and the neighborhoods that adjoin it. Until recently, this central area was the initial location—the point of attachment—for most newcomers to the city. But in addition to being the attachment point, the central area also became the staging ground from which each group sought to move to the next socio-economic level. As each group obtained more resources, its members dispersed away from the city center.

Dispersal through Chicago's South Side was accelerated and channeled by special circumstances. The Great Union Stock Yard was opened on December 25, 1865, and through the next two decades packers consolidated their slaughterhouses around this centralized marketing facility. By the 1890s only the Loop offered more jobs to prospective employees than the Stock Yard District. After the turn of the century, the development of the Central Manufacturing District near the stockyards reinforced the area's role as an employment center, making the stockyards neighborhoods a major point of attachment for many groups newly arrived in the city. And, like the central area, these community areas also became a staging ground for the upwardly mobile.

Those leaving the yards neighborhoods exited in three directions: some moved west into McKinley Park and Gage Park; others moved south into Englewood and West Englewood; and still others moved east into the southern exit corridor out of the Loop. Those who moved east intersected with those leaving the Loop area. Where these two population flows joined to the east and southeast of the yards, demand for housing and neighborhood services increased. The result was that population changes in a broad band south of the Loop were more rapid than they would have been without the presence of the stockyard workers who were drawn into that southern flowing stream of people.

The arrival of new groups in the Stock Yard and Loop areas and their dispersal from these areas constitute the fundamental demographic facts in the history of the fifteen South Side neighborhoods included in this study. Basically, these neighborhoods fall into three groups: the lakeshore communities of the Near South Side, Douglas, Oakland, Kenwood, and Hyde Park, all of which shared origins as middle- and upper- income detached suburbs; the corridor neighborhoods, including Armour Square, Grand Boulevard, and Washington Park, which also began as middle- and upper-income suburbs but which, because of excellent local transportation, were transformed into pathways for the upwardly mobile; and the stockyards neighborhoods of Bridgeport, Canaryville, Back of the Yards, Brighton Park, McKinley Park, and Gage Park, which owed their existence and character to their working-class residents, who labored primarily in the yards and Packingtown. The yards communities also differed from the other two groups because they were almost entirely "walking neighborhoods." Although the corridor and lakeshore neighborhoods had numerous amenities that could be enjoyed by the pedestrian, the livelihood and much of the social life of their residents was dependent on accessibility to the Loop; this was not the case in the stockyards areas, whose residents could afford to travel outside their neighborhoods on rare occasions only.

Several factors created additional differences in the character of life in the fifteen neighborhoods. The first was the building of railroads through the South Side. Not only did the rails form the natural boundaries for many community areas, but the Illinois Central Railroad became instrumental in the establishment of a whole string of railroad suburbs. Prairie Avenue on the Near South Side and the original subdivisions in Douglas, Oakland, Kenwood, and Hyde Park, all had their beginnings when developers opened and promoted real estate ventures connected with the Illinois Central. Farther west, other main line

carriers established freight and repair yards which provided jobs, while the Chicago Junction Railroad was closely connected with the founding and expansion of the Stock Yard and the Central Manufacturing District. The character of community life not only in the packing district neighborhoods but also in the western half of Grand Boulevard, Armour Square, and the Near South Side, as well as in eastern portions of Brighton Park and Canaryville, was set by the railroad workers who moved there in the 1850s and 1860s.

The next major factor to affect the South Side as a whole was the creation of the South Parks system, including Washington Park, Jackson Park, and the Midway Plaisance. Hyde Park gained the most—both immediately and in the long run—by the development of these parks, which began in 1869. For while it and, to a lesser extent, Kenwood, were out of the main pathway of residential migration from the north, the parks were close enough so that all those who lived there could take advantage of them. The Washington Park community first gained, then lost, from the development of the South Parks. This neighborhood was built up quickly after the parks and their adjacent boulevards were laid out, but soon thereafter an entertainment district sprang up at its southeast corner. At first the proffered amusements catered to the rich, but before the turn of the century they were transformed to attract the masses. The result was that thousands of strangers were drawn to the community, eventually making Washington Park a less desirable residential neighborhood.

The installation of urban transportation also affected the various neighborhoods in different ways. From the beginning the South Side had excellent transportation.

The first omnibus line in Chicago ran on Archer Avenue between Brighton Park Race Track and the central business district; the route of the first horsecar line in the city was along Cottage Grove Avenue; and the first elevated ran from the Loop to the South Parks, carrying visitors to the World's Columbian Exposition of 1893. The corridor neighborhoods were almost entirely shaped by the expansion of successive modes of urban transportation as developers erected apartment buildings for thousands who wanted easy access to the Loop or the yards and a way to get to recreational facilities throughout the city. The lakeshore communities also benefited from good local transport, which enhanced the advantages these areas enjoyed because of the presence of the Illinois Central Railroad.

The increased use of cars and trucks after World War II had a significant impact on the South Side neighborhoods. This was most dramatically demonstrated in the case of the stockyards areas. Economy and convenience led to a growing use of trucks and this became an important factor in the decision of the major meatpackers during the 1950s to move their operations out of Chicago and to establish slaughterhouses closer to where livestock was raised. Trucking also eased the demand for storage and manufacturing space in the Central Manufacturing District and along the South Branch of the Chicago River. The availability of automobiles gave many families the opportunity to make new choices about commuting and where and how to spend their leisure time. People now could live in the suburbs and drive to their jobs in the stockyards district or the Loop in the same amount of time that it had previously taken them to walk to work or to get there by urban transit.

INTRODUCTION

The South Side neighborhoods experienced a more direct physical effect as a result of the public effort to handle proliferating automobile and truck traffic. After World War II, Chicago began to build a modern expressway system that emphasized movement to and from the central area. This was a cause for rejoicing among Loop merchants and workers but not always good news for the residents of the South Side. To make room for the expressways, the city razed thousands of units of housing and forced tens of thousands of residents out of their homes in Armour Square, Bridgeport, McKinley Park, and Fuller Park. This abrupt and extensive demolition broke up old community patterns in neighborhoods which had managed to retain a relatively high degree of stability in spite of their aging housing stock.

Then came the large-scale public intervention of urban renewal. By the 1950s many sections of the South Side had become prime targets for the wrecker's ball. Massive urban renewal unfortunately has proven a mixed blessing. In some cases it simply resegregated the poor—who on the South Side were mostly black—into high rise public housing projects. In other cases, most notably in Hyde Park and Kenwood, urban renewal was used to give old neighborhoods a new lease on life.

The varied consequences of urban renewal demonstrate once more the importance of large institutions in shaping community life. Mercy Hospital has been on the South Side since 1851; the present University of Chicago and the Illinois Institute of Technology (originally the Armour Institute) since 1891; and Michael Reese Hospital since 1907. Although not always good neighbors, these institutions have, on the whole, had positive rather than negative effects on the areas in which they are located. During the urban renewal years their decisions to stay, erect new facilities, and use their own money plus public funds to fight off encroaching decay, proved of paramount importance. By opting to remain these institutions have become vital anchors in the neighborhood redevelopment process.

These developments and institutions are all the more important because they have provided the framework within which the South Side neighborhood succession process has taken place. That process began in the nineteenth century when Irish and German workers came to help dig the Illinois and Michigan Canal. With the consolidation of the stockyards at the end of the Civil War, more Irish and Germans plus some Swedes and persons of American birth joined them in what became the Packingtown neighborhoods. Jobs in the slaughterhouses increased rapidly after 1890, attracting new immigrants from Southern and Eastern Europe. By that time, the earliest arrivals had established firm political control, which they maintained in spite of the growing numerical predominance of those who came later. At the same time these community areas were sufficiently large geographically and contained enough new housing to allow many second- and third- generation ethnics to continue residing there, even after they had achieved family incomes that were well within the middle-class range. When blacks and Mexicans came to work in the yards in the twentieth century, especially during the two world wars, they usually found "no vacancy" signs in the yards neighborhoods. Blacks holding jobs in Packingtown therefore continued to reside in the "black belt," which first was located entirely in the Near South Side neighborhood or in segregated enclaves along the railroad lines and yards at the western edge of Douglas, Oakland, and Washington Park.

While the yards neighborhoods developed as working-class areas, the four lakeshore neighborhoods experienced a different process of development. The discrete suburbs out of which they evolved originally were peopled by American-born, Germans, and Scandinavians of the upper and middle class. By the 1880s, however, a group succession process had begun in these areas, by which newer ethnics replaced older ethnics and Catholics and Jews replaced Protestants. That changeover took place first in the Near South Side neighborhood, but after 1890 the more recent arrivals began to move into Douglas, Oakland, and then into Kenwood and Hyde Park. Since older residents shared middle-class incomes and social tastes, this changeover was accomplished with little conflict.

The same kind of group change occurred at a faster rate in the corridor neighborhoods. By the turn of the century most of the housing units in Grand Boulevard and Washington Park were apartments, and increasingly these were small "starter units" geared to young couples trying to accumulate savings and move somewhere else where they could buy a house. Ethnic change occurred rapidly in the corridor communities, probably accompanied by a slight lowering of income levels. Blacks, forced always to submit to a segregated housing market, eventually would move into these corridor neighborhood apartments because the older and newer ethnics and the American-born had moved on, leaving vacancies behind. This pattern of high mobility was especially prevalent in the blocks along the elevated line. Farther east and west, the change proceeded at a more sedate pace—families bought and sold single-family houses as their needs and income levels changed.

While Grand Boulevard and Washington Park showed the highest degree of change in the decades around the turn of the century, Gage Park and Brighton Park remained largely undeveloped. Only a few old ethnic families had moved into either of these neighborhoods by the 1890s, and most of the housing stock that presently stands there was not put up until the 1920s. The opening of most of the subdivisions in these neighborhoods is associated with the departure of upwardly mobile Poles and other Slavs from the yards neighborhoods. Although that exodus became a mass movement in the 1920s, it took another three decades for all the lots to be filled up.

So long as residents perceived the newcomers moving into their neighborhood as not very different from themselves, there were minimal frictions. But when the change involved a major difference in economic levels or when the old group regarded the newcomers as socially and culturally unassimilable, conflict ensued. Until one or the other of these events occurred, a neighborhood usually was regarded as stable, in spite of a considerable amount of movement within and between neighborhoods. A neighborhood began to be perceived as unstable whenever a group at one economic level began to move out faster than replacements of the same economic level moved in. When a group with lower family income—regardless of its ethnic or racial character—replaced a higher income group, a neighborhood came to be viewed as unstable and on the decline.

Neighborhood succession became more visible, and usually more rapid, when it involved blacks. Before the great migration of World War I, blacks were concentrated in the Near South Side, but the tens of thousands of blacks who flooded into the city in search of jobs during the war crowded into other segregated residential enclaves on the South Side. Segregation forced blacks of all classes to reside in the same areas, preventing upwardly mobile and middle-class blacks from spreading out into other, more affluent residential areas.

By the end of World War I, as whites followed a trail of upward mobility through the South Side middle-class neighborhoods, the black middle class was willing to pay more for the same kind of housing. Thus, when a previously all-white block was broken by a landlord eager to obtain higher rent or an owner who wanted greater profit, it was not hard to find black families willing to pay extra to break away from the slums. Poorer blacks, who had fewer alternatives than middle-income blacks, would also pay a premium to move into formerly all-white areas. They often financed such a move by doubling up and overcrowding, much the same way as white ethnic families did. But since the black middle class and the black poor moved in such a tight time sequence, what was actually two different processes was perceived by whites as a single one. Hence, the arrival of a single black family in a white neighborhood was viewed as tantamount to the imminent transformation of the area into a slum ghetto, a perception which too often turned into a self-fulfilling prophecy as whites anticipated the change and moved en masse. The self-interested manipulation of racial fears and hopes by some real estate owners and dealers who understood the dual nature of Chicago's South Side housing market often accelerated this racial transition.

The ethnic neighborhoods around the yards were not involved in this racial succession process before the 1970s for two reasons. First, middle-class blacks did not want to move into the yards neighborhoods because the quality of the housing was not sufficiently high and, second, poorer blacks perceived the yards area as openly hostile to their movement there. The white middle class who lived in the South Side lakeshore and corridor neighborhoods had the option of running before the change. The white ethnics of the stockyards district had fewer alternatives and were more likely to remain in their old neighborhoods even after their economic situation improved. Only during the last decade, as the ethnic neighborhoods have become less solid, has a surplus of housing unwanted by whites appeared at the eastern edge of these neighborhoods. Following the creation of that vacuum, some poorer blacks moved into the stockyards area. But even that pressure has remained minimal during the 1970s.

The histories which follow are brief case studies of how several community areas have fared in dealing with changes which have affected not only Chicago but other large American cities. Although some of them seem to have been overwhelmed by the forces of growth and decay that have always been part of American urban life, others seem to have capitalized on those same forces to improve themselves. Whether one likes the results or not, the neighborhoods have been where people have made many of the crucial personal decisions that have affected the way the city has evolved. In the process they have demonstrated what they value in American life.

(Being filled up.)

THE LOOP

Chicago could begin as a city only when the frontier was safe. After the United States purchased the Louisiana Territory in 1803, federal military leaders determined that the best way to secure the new domain was by building a line of forts, sited to control waterway transfer points. The federal government already owned the territory around the mouth of the Chicago River under a treaty concluded with the Indians in 1795. Because no new treaty had to be drawn, the authorities decided to fortify the Chicago River rather than the Calumet or the Wabash, where Indian land titles had not yet been extinguished. Chicago, therefore, began as a fort town.

The site chosen for Fort Dearborn was a slight rise on the south bank of the river, a few hundred feet west of where the sluggish stream emptied into Lake Michigan. A supply ship brought building materials across the lake, while the main body of soldiers who were to erect and staff the installation walked overland from Fort Detroit following old Indian trails. The fort was completed in 1804.

The little outpost was established well in advance of immigration from the East Coast, and during the first eight years of its exist-ence life there was dull. The isolation was broken only by the appearance of occasional visitors, traders, and explorers and the arrival and departure of Indians who came to barter with the few resident traders. That Americans did not yet control the site was proven in 1812 when, under threat of attack, the commanding officer at Fort Dearborn (acting on orders sent by his commander from Detroit), drew together his soldiers and volunteer militia as well as all women and children and started out for Fort Wayne. As this small band reached what is now the area of 18th and Calumet, the Indians attacked. Most of the soldiers and settlers were killed, some were taken captive, but a few managed epic escapes. After this massacre, the Indians burned the fort, and the Chicago area fell into a slumber once more.

The army rebuilt the fort at its former site in 1816, and the Indian traders soon returned. By 1818 ten or twelve log cabins clustered near the military post. These were occupied by civilians who were not only traders but also made their living by keeping tavern for the soldiers at the fort, manufacturing trinkets for the Indians, and providing lodging, supplies, and transport to travelers and traders who passed through on their way west. Two characteristics of the habitations of these early settlers foreshadowed the shape of the future city. First, their crude buildings served multiple purposes—as places for work, residence, and social gathering. Second, most of these cabins were clustered at Wolf Point on both banks of the North Branch while the remainder were to be found around the fort on the south bank of the main stem. Thus what later became the expanded Chicago Loop began with two centers—the fort and the forks, one at what is now the southwest corner of Wacker and Michigan (the present site of the Stone Container Building) and the other around Wolf Point.

At first growth was slow. After 1827 the prospects of the area brightened as it became likely that a canal would be dug to connect the South Branch of the Chicago with the Des Plaines, Illinois, and Mississippi rivers through the old Mud Lake Portage. Meanwhile, the opening of the Erie Canal in 1825 made Great Lakes trade easier, encouraging settlement along the southern and western shores of these lakes. At the same time a continuous line of settlement spread through the Ohio Valley, then northward up the Illinois and Wabash River valleys. As construction of the Illinois and Michigan Canal began in 1836, settlers already were filling the rich agricultural land to the south and west of Chicago. Whereas the population in 1830 had been about 50, it had risen to 4,179 by 1837 when the city was incorporated. These figures suggest that the enormous real estate speculation going on in the area had some basis in reality. But the downturn brought on by the panic of 1837 showed how outrageous land prices had become during the boom.

From the 1830s until the building of numerous bridges in the 1860s, the main stem of the Chicago River acted as a barrier inhibiting the transaction of business between the Loop and what became the Near North Side. Consequently, through the 1830s, Chicago's first retail and wholesale businesses gathered in a single strip along South Water Street. In 1833, when Chicago's first deputy postmaster John Bates, Jr. located his residence at State and Madison—the present "center" of the city—the site was so far away from the community's main activity that after only a few months, he moved back to the heart of the settlement.

This initial pattern of mixed land use ended quickly. By the mid-1840s Chicago claimed more than 12,000 residents, and with that increase came the sorting out of various business activities. Large wholesale and manufacturing establishments which began to appear in the city during that decade took over South Water Street and the South Branch of the Chicago River. The principal retail businesses moved one block south to Lake Street. Although residences still could be found on the upper floors of the mostly-wooden, balloon-frame buildings, Lake Street from Wabash to Franklin functioned as a combination North Michigan Avenue and State Street of later times. This strip contained both wholesale and retail businesses, firms which carried the latest fashions from New York, and establishments selling hardware and furniture. Although offices of professionals could be found as far south as Washington, by 1848 there was not a single market where fresh meat and vegetables could be purchased south of Randolph. The result of a legal restriction, this situation continued as the residential population spread out, with boarding houses and hotels located as far south as Monroe between State and Wells. Amidst these burgeoning businesses flourished numerous churches and schools, a combination of activities which continues to shape the character of the modern Loop.

During the 1850s and 1860s the Chicago economy boomed as the population of the city jumped from 29,963 in 1840 to 109,260 in 1850 and up to 298,977 a decade later. By 1857 the Loop—bounded on the east by Lake Michigan, on the north and west by the Chicago River, and on the south by what became Roosevelt Road—was filled. Although already the city's premier business district, this area had quite a different character from the present Loop. One difference was that it contained both slums and fashionable residences. The latter, by the mid-1850s, were especially prominent along Michigan and Wabash avenues south of Van Buren. During the same decade crude working-class dwellings were built on Clark and State streets, spreading northward from Roosevelt Road and the railroad shops and yards located at the south edge of the downtown. The worst habitations in the Loop, however, were the alley dwellings located within the stone-walled business blocks, with the fashionable facades of businesses concealing the shanties and lean-to dwellings that occupied the squalid cores. Such structures would provide excellent fuel for the Chicago fire of 1871.

Four elements characterized Loop development during the 1860s. First, new buildings constructed in this decade tended to be taller than previously. By 1870 numerous five- and six-story buildings had been erected. Most of these had retail stores on their ground floors with offices above. Second, manufacturing and wholesaling, though scattered throughout the central district, were concentrated mainly north of Randolph toward the Chicago River. Already in the 1860s, however, manufacturers were moving out of the Loop to water- and rail-oriented locations. Meanwhile, coal and lumber yards, stone-cutting firms, and warehouses pushed westward as far as Franklin and Wells along the east bank of the South Branch.

The third development began in the mid-1860s when Potter Palmer and other real estate developers recognized that Lake Street would never be able to accommodate all of the central business district's carriage-trade retail stores. Palmer led the way when he ordered the demolition on State Street of numerous single family two- and four-flat houses belonging to him. While this wooden housing was being razed Palmer erected a large business block at State and Randolph. When completed this block was leased to Field, Leiter and Company, the forerunner of Marshall Field and Company. By 1870 retail dry goods stores, supplemented by other elegant shops selling jewelry and furniture, had taken command on both sides of State between Polk and Lake. Just before the fire, then, State Street and the parallel streets of Dearborn and Clark made up a retail corridor cutting through the middle of the Loop. Thus the retail axis of the Loop shifted from east and

Looking west from the head of LaSalle Street,
1831. This rendering by an unknown printmaker
shows the Potawatomi Indians still encamped
on the south bank of the Main Stem. The
Sauganash Hotel over which Mark Beaubien
presided can be seen behind the tepees.
In the center is the Wolf Tavern and to the right
Sam Miller's Public House. CHS.

west to north and south.

The fourth development was the establishment of a single city and county government center and the beginning of the financial district. The former was the outcome of governmental action; the latter represented a response from the private sector. By 1850 both the City Council and the County Commission realized they had outgrown their separate quarters and struck a deal by which each government would have one-half of a new Cook County Court House to be erected in the public square bounded by Clark, Randolph, LaSalle, and Washington streets. The City Hall–Court House Building was opened in 1853, and, in spite of numerous attempts to move both city and county government headquarters out of their Loop locations, the two have remained there ever since except for a brief period following the fire of 1871. The private sector decision was made by the Chicago Board of Trade. Since 1848 this organization had done business at LaSalle and South Water streets. In 1865 the Board moved its exchange into new quarters at LaSalle and Washington streets.

During the 1860s the Court House block and the Board of Trade became focal points around which clustered banks, real estate and insurance agents, attorneys, architects and contractors, and the offices of advertising agents, newspapers, and telegraph companies. The rough boundaries of this governmental and financial section were Lake, Wells, Adams, and State. Overlaying this service cluster was another of a slightly different character. It comprised physicians' offices and art and music studios. The focus of this latter group was just east of the former, in the two blocks bounded by Madison and Randolph, Dearborn and Clark.

The Loop also contained numerous hotels in the 1860s. The better hotels at first were near the river, then they tended to cluster around the city's railroad stations. For the many travelers who stayed in these hotels, the Loop offered an additional amenity: by 1870 a vice district was located south of Washington and west of Wells, with its center at Wells and Monroe streets. That location was the third area occupied by the "forces of evil." Their point of origin had been the Wolf Point district; then in the 1840s, as manufacturing and wholesaling moved into that area, vice was forced into the shanties and rooming houses in the south half of the Loop. With the development of State Street, illicit activities were driven to the southwest corner of the central district.

As this sorting out process occurred, the city government mandated a number of improvements in public services. During the 1850s the grade of all streets was raised in order to provide proper drainage and sewer flow; plank and wood-block pavement was used to surface the streets, and plans were made to construct several bridges across the river. A locally chartered private company provided gas for lighting in 1850, and in 1859 newly established corporations began to operate horsecar lines. The first of these ran on State between Lake and 12th (now Roosevelt Road), from which it was quickly extended farther south. Soon after, the West Side system entered the Loop along Madison Street. North Side lines had no access to the central district before 1871. Mainline steam railroads, however, provided some transportation for North Siders by running numerous accommodation trains which allowed high income workers to live in the suburbs while working in the Loop. In the

short run cheap public transit and commuter railroads permitted easy access to the Loop and encouraged its development, but in the long run both had the effect of encouraging a dispersal of population away from the central district and eventually away from the city proper.

Loop reconstruction after the fire of 1871 demonstrated both continuity and change. The most obvious continuity was in land ownership. Despite the fact that the fire destroyed the Court House which contained all the community's official land records, enough privately held documents survived to re-establish lot boundaries. Since few owners disputed these lines, rebuilding could occur quickly. One consequence was that many owners, including Potter Palmer, used pre-fire plans to reconstruct their buildings on the same sites.

Among the most noticeable changes in the post-fire Loop was an increase in the height of buildings: many owners took the opportunity to build at least one story higher. This trend was encouraged by an innovation in building technology. Elevators had been installed in downtown office buildings during the 1860s, but the problem of devising appropriately strong frames for the taller structures still remained. Engineer William Le Baron Jenney solved the problem in his design for the Home Insurance Building (completed in 1885) by using cast iron beams to support the weight of each floor. Once the walls no longer had to bear the load, the amount of space devoted to windows could be increased. From Jenney's beginning came the innovative designs of the Chicago School of Architecture. Between 1885 and 1894 twenty-one skyscrapers (from 12 to 16 stories high), most designed in the new mode, made their appearance in the Loop, including Burnham and Root's Rookery at LaSalle and Adams.

Another significant change was the progressive diminution of residential buildings. Some of the alley dwellings were already being torn down to make way for taller structures in the 1860s. After the fire the City Council decreed that no wooden buildings could be put up in the central business district so that the residents of such pre-fire buildings were pushed out of the Loop.

During the 1880s cable car lines, serving the north, south, and west districts of the city, replaced the slower horsecars. In 1892 transportation connections to the center were again improved with the construction of an elevated steam railway that operated between Congress and 55th streets on the South Side. By 1897 both the newer elevateds and most of the streetcar lines into the Loop were being powered by the "magic lightning" of electricity.

What is not widely known is that the Loop owes its name to the earlier cable car system rather than to the ring of Chicago's elevateds which ran on Wabash, Lake, Wells, and Van Buren. Actually, the term "Loop" crept into the Chicago vernacular a decade before most of the elevateds were built. At a stockholders meeting in 1883, the president of the Chicago City Railway Company stated that "cars commenced running January 28, 1882, between 21st St. and Madison St., and a few days after that to 39th St. and also around the eight blocks north of Madison St., commonly known as the loop."*

Within fifteen years after the Chicago fire, the central district was in the midst of

* From Roy Maltbie, ed., *The Street Railways of Chicago: Report of the Civic Federation of Chicago* (Reprinted from *Municipal Affairs*, 1901), p. 55. Maltbie was one of the first scholars of the evolution of Chicago's traction system.

yet another developmental stage. The relocation of the Board of Trade from LaSalle and Washington five blocks south to LaSalle and Jackson in 1885 proved an important shift. Six years earlier, in 1879, the Chicago Post Office and Custom House, which had been located at the northwest corner of Dearborn and Monroe, reopened on the block bounded by Jackson, Clark, Adams, and Dearborn.

By the mid-1880s this triangle of buildings—the Court House–City Hall, the Board of Trade, and the Federal Building—constituted the core of the Loop's administrative, financial, and communications activities. These were carried on in the area bounded by Randolph, State, Van Buren, and Wells. Real estate agents, lawyers, life insurance companies, stock and bond brokers, banks, commission merchants, newspapers, architects, and contractors all competed for space in the multi-storied buildings which stood in this area.

The fitting symbols of this ambitious development were the impressive buildings in the LaSalle Street financial canyon. By 1886 these included the Counselman, Gaff, Mallers, Rookery, and Insurance Exchange buildings, all located in the two blocks between Adams and Jackson. The completion of the Chicago Stock Exchange Building in 1894 at the southwest corner of Washington and LaSalle tended to extend the canyon effect northward, but not without low-level interruptions. By 1900 LaSalle Street had become a regional and national financial center.

State remained the primary retail street, and not without reason. Along that street great department stores like Marshall Field, Carson Pirie Scott, and The Fair became retail magnets attracting shoppers from the whole region. During the last two decades

of the nineteenth century, the elite carriage trade began to patronize fashionable specialty shops located along Michigan Avenue south of Randolph. But while State was the primary retail market strip and Michigan was geared to the tastes of the wealthy, retailing pervaded the entire Loop. By 1910 stores were squeezed into every nook and cranny of the central business district, from restaurants and shops on the first floor of the prestigious Rookery Building to discount fabric houses on West Madison.

In the mid-1880s the Loop was also the place for culture. Nine theaters and clubs like the Iroquois, the Union League, the Athenaeum, and the Chicago, were to be found there, to say nothing of the Auditorium Building erected at the northwest corner of Michigan Avenue and Congress Street in 1889. Adjacent to it stood the Studebaker Building, later renamed the Fine Arts Building, which by 1900 had become a favored location for the studios and headquarters of architects, artists, craftsmen, musicians, publishers, and various cultural clubs. With all this competition many of the practitioners of the high arts began to move elsewhere in search of cheaper space than could be found on Michigan Avenue. A number of them ended up moving west to Clark Street between Randolph and Adams. Confirming Michigan Avenue's importance as a location for culture, The Art Institute of Chicago was constructed in 1893 at Michigan and Adams, initially as a meeting place for various congresses during the World's Columbian Exposition.

Wholesaling also continued to be important in the Loop in the 1880s but less so than during the 1860s. Before the age of the motor truck, intracity freight still had to be moved entirely by horses, so it was important that the warehouses supplying the central district retail establishments be located close to the city center. Warehousing in the Loop, therefore, made its last stand near the South Branch of the Chicago River. Henry Hobson Richardson's Marshall Field Wholesale Building was opened in 1887 on the block bounded by Wells, Quincy, Franklin, and Adams. The Ryerson Building (later known as the Walker Warehouse), designed by Louis Sullivan, was started the next year at 200–214 South Market. Richardson and Sullivan proved that massive commercial storage buildings could be beautiful as well as functional. After 1890, however, warehousing began to decline in this area and by the turn of the century had retreated to the edges of the Loop.

Chicago had hosted its first national convention in 1847 when representatives from the Northeast and West gathered in the city to develop a united response to President James Polk's veto of an omnibus rivers and harbors improvement bill. So many people attended this convention that all hotel space was filled, and thousands of visitors had to be put up in private homes. Thirteen years later Chicago hosted its first national political convention, called by the Republicans who nominated Abraham Lincoln for the presidency. Thus even before the fire of 1871 Chicago had become a convention city, and that in turn stimulated hotel construction.

By 1900 first class hotels were scattered throughout the northern two-thirds of the Loop. Those guests who had business with local or county government or in the financial center, operated from hotels on Clark Street. Shoppers could stay in hotels on State, and those interested in easy access to elegant stores and culture could choose among several along Michigan. Thus for each important cluster of goods and services offered in the Loop, the out-of-towner could find a convenient cluster of fine hostelries. In addition, activity in the area was so concentrated that each hotel was within reasonable walking distance of the others.

Transients, especially single males who could not afford the more splendid accommodations, had recourse to boarding houses in the section of the Loop extending from Van Buren to 12th Street, especially in the 1880s and 1890s. Typically the first floors of such buildings were occupied by retailers of various kinds, including cut-rate stores, cheap restaurants, penny arcades, and later, nickel theatres. A number of these businesses engaged in some form of illegal activity and, by 1900, State and Wabash between Adams and 12th Street was considered the heart of the Levee* vice district. So vicious were the thugs who preyed on the clientele of these establishments that locals dubbed the area "Little Cheyenne," after the city of that name in Wyoming, then considered the most openly wicked in the country. Within a couple of decades, in an ironic turn-around, the citizens of Cheyenne retaliated by calling their city's most disreputable section "Chicago."

The World's Columbian Exposition of 1893 had a considerable impact on the Loop even though its immediate setting was Jackson Park. Public officials and private groups of Chicagoans prepared for the fair by making the City's central district more attractive for visitors. The local government worked on streets, curbs, and sidewalks, while owners of major buildings saw to it

that the exteriors of their edifices were cleaned. Meanwhile a group of businessmen decided to do something about the disgraceful condition of the lakeside park which lay east of Michigan between Randolph and 12th. For years this area had been used as a dump where builders piled rubble at the water's edge while homeless men set up ramshackle squatters' shacks on the large open space innocent of trees or landscaping.

This group of merchants commissioned Daniel Burnham to create a design to improve the Lake Front Park at the eastern edge of the Loop. Although the plan was not completed until 1897, well after the fair, and was not acted upon even then, it became the forerunner of Burnham and Bennett's celebrated *Plan of Chicago* published in 1909 by the Commercial Club.

Businessman A. Montgomery Ward, as a property owner on the west side of Michigan, fought off all attempts to put up buildings of any kind in the open space east of that avenue. Backed by a succession of city ordinances, the first passed in 1838, Ward in 1902 won the case for Chicago's Lake Front Park (renamed Grant Park the previous year). During the first decade of the twentieth century this area was gradually transformed through grading and landscaping. The Loop's great "front porch" thus was secured and enhanced for future generations.

Many of the trends in Loop development which began in the 1870s continued into the next century. State Street retail activity expanded with the addition of retail giants like the new Boston Store, at the northwest corner of Madison Street, designed by Holabird and Roche and completed between 1905 and 1917. That expansion, combined with Mayor Carter Harrison's

---

* The name "Levee" came from Memphis and New Orleans where levee areas along the river were the principal vice districts.

Elegant residences in the Loop, December 1866. Park Row, later E. 11th Place, took its name from this elegant row of brownstones at the south end of Lake Front Park. One of the city's early apartment houses stood at the east end of the street. In the background is an Illinois Central locomotive heading north toward the Randolph Street freightyards on the company's causeway, which paralleled the shoreline. Jevne & Almini lithograph, CHS.

View west on South Water Street across Clark Street, 1866. Four- and five-story warehouses and stores had replaced the crude cabins of the pioneers in this Jevne & Almini lithograph executed shortly after the Civil War. The usual traffic congestion at this corner is intensified because the Clark Street Bridge has been opened to allow a ship to pass up the Chicago River, and hacks, drays, and carriages are backed up waiting for the bridge to close. CHS.

1905 anti-vice campaign, had the effect of pushing the vice district farther south. New hotels were built, including the palatial Blackstone on Michigan Avenue designed by Marshall and Fox. The greatest demand, however, was for office space. The federal, county, and city governments all built new administrative headquarters in the Loop between 1905 and 1911, while in the private sector Daniel Burnham's 17-story Railway Exchange Building was only one of many tall structures put up before World War I. Taller buildings replaced tall ones in a constant adaptation to changing needs and rising land values: the competition for Loop space had grown acute.

After 1909 civic leaders began to reshape the Loop according to the guidelines set forth in the *Plan of Chicago*, one of whose recommendations had been that the city build a recreational pier eastward into the lake. In 1916 the Municipal Pier (renamed Navy Pier in 1927) was opened. Served by a streetcar line the pier reached the height of its popularity in the 1920s when thousands attended concerts and displays or picnicked on its beautiful walkways. Immediately west of the pier, as part of a massive locally-funded urban renewal project also recommended in the Burnham-Bennett plan, Chicago razed the decrepit wholesale warehouses along East South Water Street and replaced them with a formal esplanade of the kind to be found in Paris and other European river cities. The demolition of the warehouses, which began in 1922, marked the end of the wholesale produce market in the Loop.

The construction of the double-decker Wacker Drive* signified the Loop's new

*   Named in honor of Charles H. Wacker who had been a key figure in the implementation of the Burnham Plan of 1909.

dependency on the automobile and motor truck. So too did the building of the two-level bridge at Michigan Avenue and the demolition of the badly sited Rush Street Bridge. This change, completed in 1923, converted Michigan Avenue into a highly effective artery from the Loop to the North Side and stimulated the development of the North Michigan Avenue shopping district between Oak Street and the river.

The same year in which the Michigan Avenue Bridge opened, a change in zoning ordinances encouraged a new construction boom in the Loop. The change not only allowed higher buildings but also encouraged the use of setback towers. Among the significant buildings to be completed under the new regulations were the 21-story Chicago Temple in 1923; the 41-story Bankers Building in 1928; the 45-story Civic Opera in 1929; and the 49-story One North LaSalle Building in 1930.

Just as significant as this construction within the old Loop was the new construction outside it. The two corporate skyscrapers which broke the confines of the Loop were the Wrigley Building (1921–1924) and the Tribune Tower (1925), both located just north of the river on Michigan. Meanwhile the erection in 1920 of the 13-story Drake Hotel at the southeast corner of North Michigan Avenue and Lake Shore Drive and the completion in 1925 of the 25-story Chicago Allerton House at 701 North Michigan indicated that the Loop alone could no longer handle the total demand for hotel accommodations. In the ensuing four years offices and stores, as well as hotels, moved outside the limits of the Loop.

Then the Great Depression struck. After 1934, following completion of the 23-story Field Building with its 19-story tower, and the 8-story Goldblatt's Store at 330-32

South Wabash, no new buildings were constructed in the Loop until the mid-1950s. Nevertheless, there were changes. During the two decades before the depression about seventy-five office buildings had been erected in this area, and by 1935 they predominated in all parts of the Loop except for the southwest quadrant. These buildings served a variety of space needs, from housing single companies like Pure Oil, to serving as headquarters for financial institutions such as London Guarantee Bank, to providing office space for several different companies, as in the case of the building at 166 West Jackson.

While the densest office development continued to be in the financial-administrative corridor, between Jackson on the south, Randolph on the north, Wells to the west, and Dearborn to the east, by the mid-1930s nearly every block in the central district had some offices. Even more than previously the office space was divided into functional clusters. Real estate brokers were most heavily concentrated in the two blocks south of the City Hall and Court House, between LaSalle and Clark, from Monroe to Washington. Lawyers clustered in the same two blocks but also in the two blocks between Wells and LaSalle and Washington and Lake. Stockbrokers naturally wanted proximity to the Stock Exchange and took offices on both sides of LaSalle between Jackson and Monroe, while grain dealers who dealt on the commodity exchange sought quarters between Van Buren and Monroe and between Clark and Wells. Professional offices followed the same pattern. Doctors, for example, were most heavily grouped along Michigan Avenue and Wabash, between Washington and Van Buren. Theaters were more scattered but could be found in discernible

Real estate company map showing rapid reconstruction after the Chicago fire. John Culver, a dealer in city and suburban real estate, published this map in 1872. In the accompanying text Culver assured prospective buyers that "only permanent structures are included . . . whether completed, or even commenced" and that "none of the shanties which disfigure the lake front" were shown. CHS.

South on LaSalle across Adams facing the Board of Trade Building, 1893. This commercial structure located at LaSalle and Jackson housed the city's commodity exchange from 1885 until 1930, when it was replaced by the present building. Architect W. W. Boyington designed the 10-story building with a 300-foot tower which had to be removed in 1895 because its great weight had caused excessive settling. The Rookery on the left and the Insurance Exchange Building on the right were among the Board of Trade's prominent neighbors. S. L. Stein gravure, CHS.

Dairy Kitchen Hotel, northwest corner of State and Madison, in the early 1890s. E. F. Dore erected this five-story business structure in 1872. The ground floor was occupied by a dry goods firm, the remaining floors were used for offices. By 1890 a restaurant-hotel firm had taken over most of the space in the building. It was razed in 1893 to make way for the 15-story Champlain Building opened the following year. CHS.

concentration along Michigan, State, and Randolph.

During the 1920s and 1930s parking lots had to be built for those who worked or shopped in the Loop. In 1927 there were 26 parking garages and 34 large parking lots in or near the Loop; ten years later there were 40 garages and 161 lots. Together, these 201 facilities, employing 1,200 people, had a peak capacity of 23,750 cars. Within the central district these parking facilities had a definite locational pattern. Most were to be found in what was, in effect, a large right-angled triangle, with Jackson and Michigan constituting the right angle and with a line drawn from Michigan and Roosevelt to Van Buren and Market as the third side. Garages and lots also were located immediately north and west of the Loop. Thus, by the mid-1930s, parking had become an important central area land use.

The parking lot and office construction boom of the 1920s put pressure on wholesalers—long part of the central district's life—to move to other areas. During the depression decade some went out of business, while those who remained found their activities hampered by traffic congestion. Wholesalers also experienced another kind of pressure because of the conversion of warehouses into office buildings which began in the 1930s. This was the case with the 16-story Butler Building at 162 North State, which had been erected as a warehouse in the 1920s. Indeed, during the 1940s, approximately one and a half million square feet of floor space were converted from warehousing and wholesaling to office use, an additional million were converted before the end of 1954. That trend continued in the 1960s and 1970s. As warehousing was being pushed from the Loop, large furniture and musical instrument stores whose traditional customers had moved farther away and whose locations had become too expensive to maintain, found themselves with insufficient business to stay in the Loop. Many of these retailing giants, especially on South Dearborn, closed their doors in the 1950s. Some reopened in suburban shopping districts, but others decided that their kind of merchandising was anachronistic and went out of business altogether.

But along with these losses came stunning gains. The 1957 opening of the Prudential Insurance Building at Randolph, east of Michigan Avenue, on air rights over the Illinois Central Railroad tracks, signaled the end of the Loop building blockade. Between 1957 and 1977, thirty million square feet of office space were added to central area stock, nearly doubling what had been available before the boom began. These enterprises included some of the buildings that have come to symbolize Chicago's downtown renaissance: Inland Steel (1957), United of America (1962), U. S. Gypsum (1963), The Brunswick (1965), First National Bank (1969), John Hancock Center (1970), and Sears Tower (1975). New hotels were added as well, including the Hyatt Regency Chicago at 151 East Wacker, the Water Tower Hyatt House at 800 North Michigan, the Ritz-Carlton at 160 East Pearson, and McCormick Inn at 23rd and Lake Shore. Moreover, the federal government, Cook County, and the City of Chicago all erected new public administration buildings in the central area.

This new volume of construction had two disturbing elements, however. The first was that much of it took place outside the traditional boundaries of the Loop, notably along Michigan Avenue on the Near North Side and across the Chicago River on the Near West Side. Although Chicago's desirable office space and convention hotels remained more centrally concentrated than in most American cities, the Loop had lost its monopoly of such functions. The second disturbing condition was that in the course of its transformation into an office center, the Loop forfeited its preeminence in fashionable retailing and entertainment. In 1950 the Loop operated round the clock; by 1970 it tended to close down after five o'clock. Furthermore, Loop retailers found themselves competing for trade with an alternative business district, North Michigan Avenue. The most optimistic conclusion that a 1976 study of central area business could draw was that North Michigan Avenue and Loop retailers were serving complementary markets—that while the presence of one shopping area tended to reinforce the existence of the other, the two had a discernibly different clientele.

Current redevelopment plans for the Loop include measures to counteract its most severe losses. As of 1978, State Street is being converted into a mall on which automobiles will be prohibited. The key to the success of this plan, if it follows patterns already apparent in other cities, is the provision of cheap parking close to the major retailers whose establishments line State Street. The other plan is more grandiose. It involves the demolition of older buildings along Randolph and the installation there of tall multiple-use buildings that would include apartments, retail stores, and offices. The main thrust of these measures is to bring residents back into the Loop so that the old central area can regain its round the clock character or can at least attract a substantial number of shoppers who will make their purchases in Loop stores. Proposals made for the Near South

Michigan Avenue at Van Buren Street between 1882 and 1884. The large building in the center is the Victoria Hotel, which stood at this location between about 1875 and 1908. At the left is the two-story Art Institute, which had changed its name from the Academy of Fine Arts in 1882. CHS.

View northwest at Michigan Avenue and Congress, 1889. In front of the Auditorium designed by Adler & Sullivan are piles of stone left over from the construction of that building. Elegant residences built in the 1870s still lined Michigan Avenue when this 10-story combination hotel, office building, and opera house was erected. CHS.

Side have the same purpose.

Unlike many residential neighborhoods, the Loop has the financial resources to carry out redevelopment. Roughly 85 percent of all funds invested in the central area renaissance of the 1960s and 1970s has come from private sources and both local and out of town investors seem willing to put additional money into the core of the city as long as the climate for profit making remains good. In addition, unlike many residential neighborhoods, the Loop has a substantial base from which to rebuild, for this particular "neighborhood" has been continuously renewing itself since it was first laid out in the 1830s. That process of renewal is still occurring, and the effort to regain its lost residential function and solidify its retail trade are only the most recent episodes in the history of Chicago's oldest and most central neighborhood.

Wholesale warehouses along the South Branch of the Chicago River, 324–332 South Market Street, October 30, 1938. These buildings featured loading docks at the river's edge and depended on wagons and later trucks to make deliveries to the retail stores in the Loop. CHS.

This gravure from the Chicago Real Estate Album of Levi Z. Leiter shows a manufacturing building at 169–71 Adams Street in the Loop in 1905 or the following year. CHS.

North on Wabash from Monroe, 1905–1910.
Until the construction of the elevated, Wabash
merchants hoped to replace their State Street
rivals as the city's preeminent retailers. The
dirt and noise introduced by the "L" put an
end to these hopes. Some civic leaders want to
tear down the Loop elevated, others see
it as a unique part of the city's history. CHS.

Remnants of the Old Loop vice district, west
side of State Street from just south of Harrison,
July 14, 1952. A burlesque theater and a pawn
shop serve as reminders that vice flourished in
this area at the turn of the century. In the
late 1950s State Street merchants believed that
they would soon be rid of these seamy relics,
but they had to wait until the 1960s–70s for the
buildings to be demolished. Photo by
J. Sherwin Murphy, CHS.

View northwest across Soldier Field, 1929.
The Field Museum of Natural History can be
seen behind the stadium and the newly
completed Shedd Aquarium is at the right.
Work is still proceeding on Grant Park. The
Michigan Avenue skyline is in the background.
Photo by Chicago Aerial Survey Company, CHS.

State Street, view north from Madison about
1940. Pedestrians crowd the sidewalks. Wher-
ever possible the drivers of motor vehicles
are taking advantage of the smooth tracks of
the electric street railway and running their
cars along them. Soon after this photograph
was taken State Street was torn up for
the installation of the subway. CHS.

View north from Roosevelt Road across the railroad yards behind the Grand Central Station, 1971. These once busy yards just south of the Loop have now been abandoned. Within the last decade this area has attracted the attention of developers whose plans would have the effect of creating an expanded Loop.
Photo by Casey Prunchunas, CHS.

Since its dedication in 1967, this 50-foot high steel sculpture designed by Pablo Picasso has been the subject of much controversy. It stands in front of the Daley Center which houses county court rooms and offices.
Photo by Betty Hulett, CHS.

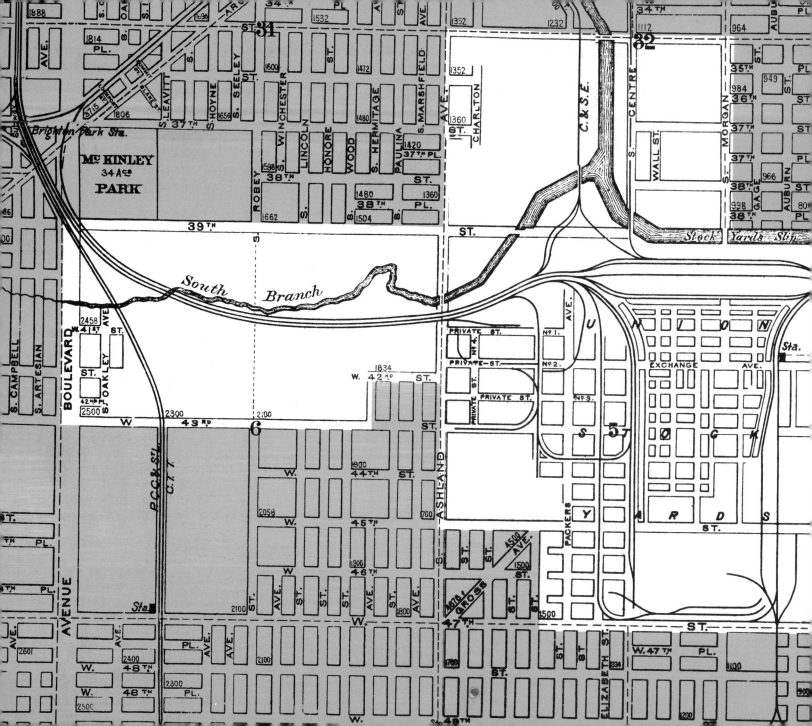

STOCK YARDS/CMD

For a hundred years the Union Stock Yards, Packingtown, and the adjacent Central Manufacturing District served as the employment center for Chicago's South Side. By the turn of the century, 47 percent of all Chicago's population resided in this division of the city. Located about three and a half miles both from Lake Michigan and the western city limits, thirty minutes by streetcar from the central business district, and with access to all areas of the city through rapid transit and surface transit, the Union Stock Yards held a position in the city's economic life second only to that of the Loop.

The trading and manufacturing processes which brought the stockyards into existence began in the Chicago area before the city was established. Fur trader Gurdon Hubbard drove a herd of cattle into Chicago in the 1820s. The animals were slaughtered and the meat sold to the Fort Dearborn provisioner and to the settlement's handful of citizens. In 1829 Archibald Clybourne established the first butchering plant on the North Branch of the Chicago River a short distance above Wolf Point. By the early 1860s seven stockyards existed in the Chicago vicinity, ranging in size from 15 to 40 acres,

while numerous packinghouses had located along the South Branch in Bridgeport. In 1861 Chicago surpassed Cincinnati in the number of hogs slaughtered annually. The Civil War brought more meat packers to the young metropolis as they fled the war zone. Once here, they found the arrangements for stock purchasing inconvenient because their buyers had to travel around to the different yards where prices and quality varied. And after the stock was purchased, it had to be driven through the streets to the packinghouses on the Chicago River.

Agitation for the creation of one large stockyard where all the city's livestock business could be carried on in an efficient manner began during the Civil War. Leading the movement was the Chicago Pork Packers Association which in June 1864 called for the establishment of a Union Stock Yard. The *Chicago Tribune* quickly gave editorial support to the idea. Nine different railroads which transported livestock into the city also backed the proposal for one consolidated yard. The Union Stock Yard and Transit Company was established to implement the plan. The company purchased 320 acres of swampland from a former mayor, "Long John" Wentworth, for $100,000, devised an

ingenious method for draining the area, built the yards, and laid the rails of the Chicago Junction Railroad which connected the yards with all the main line railroads entering the city. The "Great Union Stock Yard," as it was called by many, opened on Christmas Day 1865. The facility then contained pen space for 21,000 cattle, 75,000 hogs, 22,000 sheep, and 200 horses. A few days after the new yards began operation, the seven stockyards owned by the railroad lines were closed.

Until the mid-1870s Chicago packinghouses remained at their locations along the South Branch of the Chicago River, east of Halsted. Then new, expanded plants began to rise in the district immediately west of the yards' pen area. Located between the growing urban centers of the East and the rich livestock producing areas of the West and Midwest and attached to both by an expanding railroad network, the city's stockyards grew rapidly. In 1866, the first full year of operation, the consolidated yards handled 1,564,293 head of stock. By 1900 that number had reached 14,622,315, and twenty-four years later an all-time high of 18,643,539 head. Between 1864 and 1900, meanwhile, the original 320 acres increased to 475 acres, while "Packingtown" grew to cover an additional 145 acres. By the turn of the century the yards had pen space for 75,000 cattle, 50,000 sheep, 300,000 hogs, and 5,000 horses. While these figures indicate capacity, an even more dramatic indication of the scale of the operation is to be found in the table noting the record volume of the different kinds of livestock traded in a single day. Spanning a quarter of a century, the figures are:

Cattle	November 16, 1908	49,126
Calves	September 4, 1934	10,673
Hogs	December 15, 1924	122,749
Sheep	October 16, 1911	71,792
Horses	August 7, 1916	3,036

While the consolidation of the stockyards and the expanded railroad facilities quickly made Chicago the leading livestock market in the country, the city's leadership in the slaughtering of animals, especially in the production of beef, was not assured until the development of the refrigerated railroad car. As early as 1868 the G. H. Hammond Company shipped beef in an insulated, ice-filled car, the first packer to do so. Then, in the 1870s, Gustavus Swift began experimenting with mechanical refrigeration. Following the development of a reliable unit, both the Swift and Armour companies began to manufacture and sell the cars to other packers. The railroads, fearing revenue losses, at first refused to carry the new "reefers" filled with dressed meat, but the Grand Trunk line broke the blockade. As others followed its lead, refrigerated cars became the basis for Chicago's nationwide domination of the packing industry. This technological innovation also gave Windy City packers control over the fruit-carrying trade and the hauling of other kinds of perishable goods.

The growth of the stockyards and Pack-ingtown translated into employment ranging from white collar office jobs, through various levels of skilled work on the packing lines, down to casual day labor. By the turn of the century 32,000 workers were employed in Packingtown. That number rose to more than 40,000 during World War I. When operating near capacity the stockyards required an additional 1,000 to 1,500 workers, most of them unskilled. Work in Packingtown was neither pleasant nor highly paid but generations of new immigrants found their first employment opportunities there.

Almost all of the stockyard and slaughterhouse workers lived in the neighborhoods immediately adjacent to Packingtown and therefore shared many common concerns. Eventually attempts were made to organize the workers into a union. The Knights of Labor were the first to try to enter the slaughtering plants. Their 1886 strike was unsuccessful, however, both because of weak union leadership and because the packers agreed on common action to defeat the organizing effort. Butchers walked out of the plants in 1894 as a gesture of solidarity with the Pullman Palace Car Company strikers. The ensuing riots, during which some refrigerator cars were burned, brought the United States Army to protect the plants and extend martial law to the surrounding neighborhoods.

In 1900 the Amalgamated Meat Cutters and Butcher Workmen were successful in obtaining a union contract from the packers covering skilled workers, but an effort to cover the unskilled once more provoked concerted action from the packers and in 1904 the union was broken. The Amalgamated returned to the plants during World War I but lost another major strike in the winter of 1921–22. Unionization then disappeared from the yards until a newly organized CIO union, the United Packinghouse Workers of America, brought permanent organization to the packing plants in the late 1930s. The UPWA merged with the previously established Amalgamated Meat Cutters in 1968.

Unionization, however, could not stave off the changes in butchering and transportation technology that eventually forced the Chicago stockyards to close. In 1952 the Chicago-based packer, Wilson & Company, opened a new Kansas City plant to replace an older one. The old packinghouse had consisted of several buildings with more than a million square feet of floor space covering 13 acres. The new one achieved the same production in the confines of a two-story building covering only a single acre. The butchering functions which formerly had taken up two floors now were carried out in a single 50 by 80 foot room. Compounding the potential impact of this change was a shift from railroad to motor truck transportation. Some forty years earlier, as the federal interstate highway system was being constructed, meat packers found themselves with an ever-expanding choice of plant sites. Then, through the first half of the century, the location of animal raising shifted westward, making it necessary to haul animals farther than before for butchering in Chicago.

Yet another advantage was lost by Chicago as the result of a change in the organization of animal marketing. By the 1930s packers were sending their own buyers into the countryside to deal directly with farmers and feed lot owners instead of bidding for livestock in an open market through commission agents who brought buyer and seller together. By purchasing directly from the farmer, packers eliminated the need for large stockyards. The impact of direct sell-

Union Stock Yard Gate, 1874. This wooden triple-arched gate at the corner of Exchange and Peoria avenues was replaced in 1879 by the well-known Stone Gate designed by Burnham and Root. The latter, now a historical landmark, retained the original three-arch design but also included a two-story watchman's building. *Land Owner*, January 1874, CHS.

Market Room in a Chicago packinghouse, 1892. After the animals were slaughtered by a veritable army of men, the carcasses were stored in large coolers until they were sent off to retail butchers. From A. Wittemann, *Views of the Chicago Stock Yards and Packing Houses* (1892), CHS.

ing was felt in Chicago immediately. Between 1890 and 1933 annual receipts at the Union Stock Yard had never fallen below 13,000,000 animals per year. After 1933 they never reached that figure again.

Had none of these changes occurred, the packinghouses of Chicago would still have faced serious problems after World War II. For the most part the buildings of Packingtown had been erected early in the century. In the meantime land in the central city had risen in value and tax rates had escalated. The increasing toughness of antipollution laws contributed to the packers' problems and added one more incentive for them to leave Chicago. In 1955 Wilson & Company became the first of the big packers to close its Chicago plant. Within five years all the major butchers had left the city and Packingtown became a blighted area of buildings for which no new use could be found.

The Union Stock Yard and Transit Company attempted to initiate a new era by undertaking an impressive modernization program that included the construction of a new hog house and the installation of a modern rail shipping facility. At the same time the company handed the northern part of the yards over to its sister company, the Central Manufacturing District, for industrial development.

The Central Manufacturing District traced its origins to 1890, when a group of Eastern capitalists, incorporated as the Chicago Junction Railways and Union Stock Yards Company, purchased the capital-hungry Union Stock Yard and the belt line railroad that connected with all the major trunk lines into the city. In 1902 the New Jersey Company—as this group of investors came to be known—started to acquire land parcels in what would soon be called the Central Manufacturing District.

Within three years CMD plans were fully articulated. Not only did the New Jersey Company sell or lease land like a traditional real estate company, but it constructed buildings which other companies could either rent or purchase with low down payments and long-term financing. Thus the CMD provided growing enterprises that were short of capital with needed expansion space and the opportunity to obtain new floor space without a heavy monetary outlay. Because the principal objective of these real estate development efforts was to add to the tonnage carried by the Chicago Junction Railway, the management company limited its profits in the District by keeping selling prices and rental rates low and providing an attractive package of amenities and services to prospective tenants. If the CMD managers determined that a company seeking to locate in the District was badly undercapitalized, had a tradition of bad labor relations, or would not be a heavy Chicago Junction Railway user, they kept the firm out. The Central Manufacturing District thus became a community of manufacturers as discriminating as any exclusive residential neighborhood about potential newcomers.

By 1915 the CMD's original 265-acre tract, dubbed the "East District" by the company, was completely filled. What had begun as Bridgeport's old Cabbage Patch became a thriving industrial community of one hundred companies. As the East District—which lay between 35th and 39th, with Morgan on the east and Ashland on the west—filled up, the New Jersey Company purchased another tract, this one fronting on 39th from Ashland to Western. The southern boundary of this parcel was the classification yards of the Chicago Junction Railway, so that each piece of frontage

along 39th had a generous depth of 700 feet behind it. Acting as its own promoter, the New Jersey Company came up with the title of "The Magnificent Mile" to designate this new industrial development, because it stretched an entire mile between Ashland and Western. There was more than a touch of irony in the title, however, because the tract contained the notorious Bubbly Creek, which was an open sewer for the packers. Since there was little current in the "creek" which emptied into the South Branch, it became a coagulated mass of effluent flushed into the waterway by the slaughterhouses. While construction on 39th Street (later known as Pershing Road) started in 1916, the CMD and the Sanitary District did not undertake the task of filling in some parts of noxious Bubbly Creek until the early 1920s.

World War I changed the course of the CMD's planned industrial community development when a number of buildings were constructed there for the Army Quartermaster Corps.

In 1919, with the Pershing Road tract nearly filled, the CMD management purchased the 90-acre Kedzie Development, an area bounded by Kedzie and Central Park and by 47th and 49th streets. A building innovation distinguished this development from the two earlier ones. By this time Henry Ford had successfully pioneered "straight-line production," and in the Kedzie tract, the CMD kept land costs sufficiently low to allow construction of one-story buildings in which modern assembly line techniques could be used. In 1925 the CMD expanded beyond the state by purchasing a 300-acre tract in the city of Los Angeles for development of an industrial district there. At this time the Chicago CMD had 200 buildings with a total capital invest-

Dexter Park Pavilion, shown ca. 1900, was constructed in the 1880s as part of the Dexter Park Race Track complex named in honor of a great racehorse. A market, at which horses for a variety of uses from racing to farming were traded, adjoined the pavilion. CHS.

Central Time Station Union Stock Yard, 1904. Between 7:00 AM and 8:00 AM of each working day hundreds of men gathered at the entrances to the various packinghouses in the hope of being hired. The existence of this pool of unemployed workers depressed wages in the industry. Those who were chosen would line up at the time stations and "punch in" for the day. This photograph was taken after the first 1904 meatpackers' strike had been settled. A second strike began the same day when many of the union leaders were not hired back by the superintendents. *Chicago Daily News* photo, gift of Field Enterprises, CHS.

Wrigley Chewing Gum Factory, 1915. Three years earlier the William Wrigley Company had moved its plant from Van Buren and Halsted on the near West Side to a four and a quarter-acre tract in the Central Manufacturing District. The company occupies the same site today. From a letterhead in *The Central Manufacturing District,* **1915, CHS.**

ment of more than $50,000,000 and floor area of 15,000,000 square feet.

The Great Depression brought hard times to the CMD manufacturers. The real estate company abated rents and even gave credit to its tenant companies to keep some of them in business. In what seemed a heroic profession of faith in the future, the CMD in 1931 purchased the Crawford tract. Located a short distance west of the Kedzie Development it contained 400 acres bounded on the east by Crawford Avenue (Pulaski Road), on the north by the Illinois-Lakes-to-Gulf Waterway, on the west by the Belt Railway, and on the south by an irregular line that ran along 43rd, 44th, 45th, and 47th. Departing from the method of development used for the Kedzie tract, the CMD managers did not lay everything out in advance but waited until they had a contract in hand before starting to build. Thus the development of the tract did not become fixed until firms had specified their needs and were sited. No further land was acquired by the CMD until the early 1960s, when the real estate company took over that area of the Union Stock Yard north of Exchange Avenue. After the closing of the stockyards in August 1971, the remaining pen area was turned over to CMD as the Donovan Industrial District.

In addition to being the national center for the cattle trade and the site of an early planned industrial district, the Union Stock Yard area has traditionally played a role in hosting conventions. As early as 1870 the area provided facilities for large meetings. The Dexter Park Race Track, established at that time, flourished until the 1890s, when city-wide betting scandals caused the City Council to close down all race tracks inside the city limits.

Just north of the Dexter Park Race Track was the Dexter Park Pavilion, used for showing horses and other livestock. Such shows had a long history in Chicago. Fat Cattle fairs were held on the lakefront in what became Grant Park in the 1850s, and two decades later the Illinois Department of Agriculture established a Fat Stock Show that was held annually in the Exposition Building erected in 1873 at Michigan and Adams on the front porch of the Loop. When this structure was demolished in the early 1890s, the show sponsors looked for a new home. After their efforts to find a new location failed, the meat packers undertook sponsorship of the show as a means of improving their relations with producers. The Dexter Park Pavilion having been destroyed by fire in 1899, a new brick stock pavilion was erected in time to house the first International Live Stock Exposition in December 1900. Promoters of the event dubbed the structure the "International Amphitheatre," although locals continued to use its old name for many years.

When fire swept through the stockyards in May 1934, the Amphitheatre burned down. The present building of that name erected to replace it attracted a variety of events for mass audiences. Responding to the decline in livestock trading after 1945, the management of the Amphitheatre installed air conditioning and did extensive remodeling. These improvements made the building sufficiently attractive to capture both the Republican and Democratic conventions in 1952 as well as numerous other kinds of conventions and shows. The Amphitheatre continued to be Chicago's principal convention center until the completion of McCormick Place in 1960. After the latter burned down in 1967, the Amphitheatre experienced a brief flurry of popularity and provided the setting for the Democratic Convention of 1968. Its use since then has been too infrequent to guarantee its future.

With the stockyards and Packingtown now all but gone, various proposals have been put forth for redevelopment of the vacant area. One, recently rejected, was for the creation of a large shopping center. Others call for the installation of light industrial plants of the type now located in the former pen area north of Exchange and east of Racine Avenue. Previous uses have left their mark on the landscape, however. The old plants had deep cellars which have been filled in, but this land still settles, making construction of any substantial building difficult. Although recently developed technological solutions to these construction problems promise a new lease on life for the old Packingtown district, it is unlikely that this area will ever again employ anything like the 40,000 people who worked in Packingtown at its peak.

North End of the Union Stock Yard, ca. 1924.
The yards were at the peak of their activity
when this aerial view was taken. Packingtown,
which had employed nearly 60,000 workers
during World War I, can be seen along the
lower part of the photograph; the hog market
is at the center of this picture. Photo by
Kaufmann & Fabry, CHS.

Donovan Industrial Park, 1977. This section of the Union Stock Yard south of Exchange Avenue was closed on August 1, 1971. The pen area and the Exchange Building were demolished and replaced by the Donovan Industrial Park, named after James F. Donovan, a trustee of the Central Manufacturing District. Photo by Glen E. Holt, CHS.

View southeast across the Pershing Road development of the CMD, ca. 1936. Thirty-ninth Street cuts through this aerial photograph, separating the "Magnificent Mile" of the CMD from McKinley Park. Behind the Pershing Road tract are the Chicago Junction Railroad yards, at the upper left is Packingtown. From the Central Manufacturing District's *Speaking of Ourselves* (1936).

NEAR SOUTH SIDE

The boundaries of the Near South Side are Lake Michigan on the east; the South Branch of the Chicago River, Federal and Clark on the west; Roosevelt Road on the north; and 26th Street on the south. These boundaries are more arbitrary than those of many Chicago neighborhoods because the Near South Side is a set of enclaves and transportation access routes to the Loop rather than a separate and identifiable entity.

When Chicago was incorporated as a city in 1837, over one-half of the Near South Side—the part lying between Roosevelt and Cermak—was included within the original boundaries. But most of the present community area was far from the built-up section and the Henry B. Clarke House, built in 1836 near what is now 16th and Michigan, was then a country mansion, not even suburban in the modern sense of that word. Only a few other residences dotted the area over the next decade and a half.

When railroads entered Chicago from the east and south during the 1850s, the area took on new life. For a time the Illinois Central formed its eastern border, and what became the Chicago, Rock Island & Pacific, and the New York Central lines constituted the western edge. To serve the South Loop terminals the railroads built freight yards in the western half of the neighborhood between Cermak and Roosevelt. These yards, with their adjacent manufacturing plants and warehouses, reinforced the early character of the area in which they were developed.

Irish, German, and a few Scandinavian immigrants in the 1830s and 1840s had put up a collection of cheap wooden cottages southwest of the Loop. At first these people were employed principally in work on the Illinois and Michigan Canal, but after the railroads came into the area some of them sought jobs in the yards and nearby plants. By the 1850s this section sported a name that reflected its character—The Patch—or to underscore its heavily Irish character, Conley's Patch, after a well-known matriarch in the neighborhood. The original boundaries of the Patch were from Roosevelt Road on the north to 16th on the south, with State Street on the east and Halsted on the west. "Tough" and "poor" were the words that contemporaries used to describe the denizens of this enclave.

A different type of development was stimulated by the opening of the South Side horsecar line on State Street in 1859. Extended and broadened in the early 1860s, this system provided the Near South Side with excellent local transportation. During the Civil War a number of wealthy families built large houses—some of which might more appropriately be described as mansions—along Indiana, Michigan, and Wabash. State Street served as a dividing line, with new homes for working-class families going up to the west of that important artery. But in general population density on the Near South Side remained light; neither the well-to-do nor the less prosperous expanded rapidly in their respective segments of this neighborhood.

The fire of 1871 did not burn through the Near South Side. Its point of origin was west of the river, the wind was blowing in a north-easterly direction, and the railroad yards served as a large open space to protect the area. Nevertheless, the fire changed the course of its history. Many Loop firms had to find temporary locations while the central business district was being reconstructed, and in doing so they transformed South Wabash from a residential into a commercial street. When business returned to the reconstructed central district some years later the old mansions on Wabash were converted into rooming houses and small neighborhood shops.

Another side effect of the fire was that some of the gamblers and prostitutes moved from the southwest corner of the Loop to South State between 16th and Polk. Further change occurred after the fire of 1874—which did what the holocaust of 1871 had not done—completely burned the eastern half of the Patch. The South Side railroads, needing more room for yards and freight facilities, quickly absorbed that space. The construction of the Dearborn Street Station in 1885, of Chicago's Grand Central Depot in 1891, and the LaSalle Street Station in 1903, ratified this expansion. Blacks lived on the South Side from the 1840s onward. During the next two decades about 80 percent of Chicago's black population resided in the area. In 1860 that amounted to a little more than 750 persons. During the mid-1880s about 450 Italians lived in the area between Clark and State, Taylor and 12th streets, their largest concentration in the city.

At about the same time Chicago's elite families were settling down just a few blocks east, on Prairie Avenue between 16th and 22nd streets. The first houses erected by the "Prairie Avenue Set" had been built just after the fire of 1871. It did not take long for the lots lining the four blocks of this prestigious area to be filled up. When South Michigan Avenue became a boulevard in the 1880s several stockyard millionaires chose to build their mansions there. Nevertheless, the Prairie Avenue neighborhood remained "the acme of fashionable residential streets" through the 1880s and early 1890s. The four blocks between 16th and 22nd were lined with more than fifty mansions, including the homes of Granger Far-

well, George M. Pullman, John J. Glessner, W. W. Kimball, Clarence Buckingham, Philip D. Armour, and Marshall Field Senior and Junior.

As Prairie Avenue was reaching its high point as a residential area, the developments which would lead to its decline were already under way. First, during the 1880s, cables replaced horsecars as far south as 39th Street. Second, between 1887 and 1889, a new east-west horsecar line was installed on 26th Street, intersecting with the South Side cable. Finally, between 1890 and 1892, the steam powered "Alley Elevated" was built between State and Wabash, extending from Congress to 39th. If the steam railroads are included, the Near South Side after 1890 was cut through by nearly a dozen transportation lines.

This rich transportation catalyzed a number of developments. Anticipating that the Columbian Exposition of 1893 would stimulate rapid growth, builders erected numerous apartments and residences in as yet undeveloped areas of the Near South Side. But the hoped for boom did not materialize in the immediate area, and neighborhood developers were left with a residual of high quality housing stock that could not be filled. Real estate dealers saw the opportunity to populate these buildings by opening a new housing market for middle class blacks. Thus the 1890s saw the beginning of a middle and upper class black district in the Near South Side.

Another kind of pressure was also increasing. As Loop office and retail functions took over more space, wholesale and warehouse activities had to find new locations. This need was satisfied by the erection of numerous small shops and several large multiple-story loft warehouses, extending eastward to State from the South

Branch of the river. Land-intensive retail firms also were moving south from the Loop. In 1902 the first Michigan Avenue automobile agency, attracted by the broad paved street, opened its doors near 14th. This dealership became the forerunner of the South Michigan Avenue automobile row. Interspaced with such agencies were a large number of retail furniture stores which also opened on Michigan between 12th and 16th streets. Finally, during the first decade of the twentieth century, the corner of Cermak and Prairie, now marked by the huge Lakeside Press complex of R. R. Donnelley & Sons Co., became one of the major focal points for the city's printing industry.

To serve the increasing population numerous small businesses opened up in the community area. One principal center for retail shops and restaurants was on Wabash on either side of Cermak Road. During the first decade of the twentieth century, another kind of business followed. Starting in 1905 the city began a campaign to move vice out of the Loop. "From Twentieth Street south on Michigan Avenue in sections, and in Wabash Avenue and State Street, vice reigns openly and supreme," an observer wrote. Where Cermak intersected these streets, "the forces of darkness" centered. Although this vice district was officially shut down in 1912, the area remained a secondary entertainment district.

All these developments, combined with the heavy traffic generated by the street and steam railroads and horse-drawn freight, diminished the desirability of the Near South Side as a residential area for the upper class. The exodus of the Prairie Avenue families to the Near North Side, made fashionable by Potter Palmer, began in the mid-1890s. In the course of the next ten years the magnificent houses on Prairie

PRAIRIE AVENUE.

LOUIS WAHL

EDSON KEITH

A. A. DEWEY.

DAN'L M. THOMPSON.

C. M. HENDERSON.

GEO. M. PULLMAN.

ROBERT LAW.

MARSHALL FIELD.

Drawn by Louis Braunhold.

Engraved by J. M. Wing & Co.

THE HOMES OF CHICAGO.—RESIDENCES OF PROMINENT CITIZENS ON PRAIRIE AVENUE.

Montage of elegant houses on Prairie Avenue, 1874. Set on landscaped 100-foot lots, many such houses were to be found between 16th and 20th streets. South of that the lots tended to shrink to 50 feet, though the houses remained large. Row houses began to appear between 22nd and 23rd, where the Cottage Grove streetcar line intersected Prairie. An Illinois Central Railroad stop was located at 16th and Prairie. *Land Owner*, May 1874, CHS.

WESTCHESTER PUBLIC LIBRARY
CHESTERTON, IN

were subdivided into small apartments. Later still, most were demolished altogether to make way for single-story warehouses and buildings to house light industry. Only a handful remained to become the nucleus of the Prairie Avenue Historic District designated in late 1973.

These changes were accompanied by shifts in population. The American-born and those of Irish and German nativity left the Near South Side and were replaced by groups just getting their start in America. By 1910 a discernible Italian colony had settled in the Federal Street tenements south of Cermak Road. Fifteen years later the Italian settlement on the South Side was substantial, although its center had moved farther west out of the district. With the heavy migration of blacks to the city what became known as Chicago's "black belt," a narrow corridor which ran south along South Park, Wabash, Michigan, and Indiana, began to take shape.

Despite the conversion of old houses into apartment buildings, the construction of wholesaling facilities on the Near South Side after 1900 led to a dramatic loss of population between 1930 and 1940, when the number of those living in the area dropped from 10,416 to 7,308. However, the proportion of black residents remained relatively stable at about 25 percent of the total. The influx of war workers soon after, which swelled the number of residents to 11,317, led to profound changes in the area.

Among other things, this large increase in population was not matched by a similar rise in housing stock—only 500 units being added during this period. Heavy population pressure on an area of limited and small-sized living units inevitably led to severe overcrowding as hard-pressed blacks sought housing in a segregated market. In-

exorably the population fell prey to the associated ills of poverty and crime. By all contemporary accounts the Near South Side in 1950 was "a massive social jungle."

The initial attempt to eliminate slums and improve the quality of housing in the community area was the construction, in 1955, of the Harold L. Ickes Homes by the Chicago Housing Authority. Located on an 18-acre site at 22nd and State, this project consisted of six 7-story and seven 15-story buildings. Together, they furnished 799 new dwelling units.

The existence of this housing project affected the composition of the population of the Near South Side in two ways. By 1960, two-thirds of all children in the community resided in the Ickes Homes and nearly all the families who lived there were black. Thus, while furnishing new housing units, the public housing project put a strain on schools which during the prior decade had been losing students, and reinforced the concentration of blacks in the community area.

The population and economic profile of the Near South Side could change dramatically over the next decade if projects started and proposed come to full development. Dubbed the South Loop area in the last decade, the abandoned railroad property has come to be viewed by developers as having the potential to become a cluster of self-contained communities with their own schools, recreational facilities, and numerous access routes to the Loop by public transit. Such communities could become a southern residential anchor for a revitalized Loop.

In 1977 approval was given by the city for the development of the Dearborn Park project to be erected on a portion of the former railroad land bounded by Clark,

Polk, State, and 15th streets. Several months after this project was given the go-ahead, what became known as the River City development group sought approval for a high rise project just west of the Dearborn Park tract. This complex was to comprise 11,000 units within a series of honeycomb towers not unlike the Marina City office and condominium complex. Although the City Planning Commission approved the Dearborn Park project, it raised various objections to the River City plan. Chief among these was the claim that the high population density of River City would put an unbearable strain on city services in the area. As plans for River City were mothballed, development of Dearborn Park began.

There is one other area which the scholars who originally defined Chicago communities designated as part of the Near South Side—the group of three public buildings located at the south end of Grant Park. It includes the John G. Shedd Aquarium, the Field Museum of Natural History, and the Adler Planetarium and Astronomical Museum.

The oldest of the buildings, the Field Museum, traces its origin back to the World's Columbian Exposition of 1893. At the close of that fair, Edward Ayer, a prominent community leader, approached Marshall Field and asked him for $1,000,000 to establish a permanent home for exposition exhibits. With Field's backing, the old Palace of Fine Arts in Jackson Park left over from the fair was reopened in 1894. Extensive remodeling proved inadequate to the task of staving off the progressive deterioration of what had been intended from the start as a temporary structure. Soon after the turn of the century planning for a new building began. Following the publication in 1909 of the *Plan of Chicago*, Field hired

Goss & Phillips Sash Door and Blind Manufacturing Company, southwest corner of 12th and Clark, 1873. Goss & Phillips developed a large construction supply firm after the fire of 1871. This plant, one of two owned by the company, was located to take advantage of excellent railroad connections. The yards of the Michigan Southern were immediately to the west, while the freight house of the Rock Island was just across Clark Street. *Land Owner*, April 1873, CHS.

its principal author, Daniel Burnham, as the architect for the new building.

In the *Plan of Chicago*, Burnham had included the new museum as a centerpiece for Grant Park, but until 1912 the Field Museum trustees continued to make plans to rebuild on the old site in Jackson Park. At that point the South Park Commissioners offered them a new site on reclaimed land at the south end of Grant Park. The trustees accepted it and construction began in 1913.

The design for the museum building followed the mandate laid down by Field—that it should resemble its predecessor. The latter had been modeled after the Erechteum on the Acropolis in Athens and like its original sported a Porch of the Maidens. So does Burnham's building, which was completed in 1920.

The Field family has continued its close association with the museum to this day, and has donated more than $20,000,000 to it. In 1943 the family requested that the name of the institution be changed to Chicago Museum of Natural History, but in 1966 its original name was restored.

The second building in the Near South Side cultural group is the Adler Planetarium and Astronomical Museum, which opened in 1930. Built at a cost of $1,000,000 donated by Max Adler, a former Sears, Roebuck executive, the twelve-sided structure was designed by architect Ernest A. Grunsfeld, Jr. Although its roof line suggests that the building is an observatory, the dome actually covers a centrally located viewing theater in which a computer can recreate the exact position of the earth's heavenly bodies from 1900 B.C. to the present as well as projecting their location in the future. The Association of Federal Architects has included the Adler Planetarium on its list of the nation's thirty-four most original and beautiful buildings.

The John G. Shedd Aquarium, named after its donor (a former president of Marshall Field and Company), also was opened to the public in 1930. Its design, inspired by classical Greek architecture, was executed by the architectural firm of Graham, Anderson, Probst & White. At the time of its completion this $3,500,000 building was the largest aquarium in the world, housing tanks with a capacity of two million gallons of water brought from various seas to provide appropriate environments for a wide assortment of aquatic life.

Adjacent to this cluster of cultural institutions is yet another public structure that has played an important part in the life of the city. Completed in 1926, Soldier Field was designed by the firm of Holabird and Roche which had to devise some way of harmonizing the lines of the giant stadium with those of the classically styled Field Museum. By the time it was finished the stadium had cost the Park Commissioners just under $8,000,000. Numerous spectacles and entertainments have been held there but the largest crowd ever to assemble at the stadium came for a solemn purpose. In September 1954, Soldier Field provided the setting for a gathering of 260,000 Roman Catholics who had come to celebrate the Marian year. More recently, increasing maintenance problems have led to pressures for the replacement of Soldier Field by a more modern stadium.

The Near South Side thus continues to be a community area with astonishing contrasts. While large areas of open land remain unused, Chicago's newest neighborhood, the Dearborn Park project, is taking shape in an old railroad yard. East of there, the Prairie Avenue Historic District has gained official status as well as some financial support, and its backers are making an ardent effort to recapture its faded beauty. Farther east still, across the Illinois Central tracks, Soldier Field displays the ravages of age, but its neighbors, the Field Museum, the Adler Planetarium, and the Shedd Aquarium flourish as cultural centers.

Farther south, Chicago's major convention center, McCormick Place, first erected in 1960 and rebuilt after it burned down in 1967, is expanding, taking over an abandoned warehouse nearby. Still, the Illinois Central Railroad tracks and the South Shore Drive continue to act as a barrier separating the public portions of the community area from its residential sections. From the outset to the present the Near South Side has never achieved the lineaments of a unified community, and the redevelopment now in progress follows the piecemeal pattern of the area's original development.

The fact that the Near South Side remains rich in public transportation and offers easy access to highways will aid substantially in the rejuvenation of the area, whatever specific form that takes.

Interior of the Pullman House at 18th and
Prairie Avenue. An article in *Elite*, June 1886,
noted that "The home of Mr. and Mrs. George
M. Pullman is undoubtedly the most notable
social center in Chicago." The building was
razed shortly after Mrs. Pullman's death in
1921. Photo gift of Mrs. C. Phillip Miller, CHS.

In 1889 the Standard Club, organized twenty
years earlier by a group of German Jews,
moved into this handsome building on 24th and
Michigan. By 1900 it had become one of the
wealthiest clubs in Chicago as well as one of
the largest Jewish clubs in the country. From
The Chicago Clubs Illustrated (1888), CHS.

Two-story residential buildings at 2340–2344 South Wabash, June 1916. These buildings, erected in the 1870s, were already showing signs of deterioration before the Great Migration of blacks to Chicago during World War I put new pressure on this South Side neighborhood. With no alternative housing possibilities many blacks were forced to move into buildings such as these, sometimes paying exorbitant rents for the privilege. CHS.

Southwest corner of State and 20th streets, mid-1890s. This elegant apartment building owned by prominent Chicago merchant, Levi Z. Leiter, was built during the 1890s on a site formerly occupied by a carriage factory. Levi Z. Leiter Real Estate Album, CHS.

Building at 2441–43 South Michigan Avenue, decade prior to World War I. An automobile agency and a taxicab and livery service were to be found in this building during the period of transition from horse-powered to gasoline-powered vehicles. Photo by W. A. Pridmore, CHS.

Colosimo's Night Club and Restaurant at 2130 South Wabash was opened in 1914 by "Big Jim" Colosimo, allegedly Chicago's first gang boss. Known as the "Methuselah of Chicago Cabarets" it was put on the auction block in 1947. When this photograph was taken six years later, the famous Chicago night spot had been boarded up. Photo by J. Sherwin Murphy, CHS.

DOUGLAS

The community area of Douglas has a more stable early history than its northern neighbor, the Near South Side, but the end results have been the same. The present community area of Douglas is bounded on the east by Lake Michigan, on the north by 26th Street, on the west by Federal Street and the railroad tracks of the Chicago, Rock Island & Pacific Railroad, and on the south by a line running west from Lake Michigan along 35th Street to Vincennes, then southwest on Vincennes to 39th, and west on 39th to Federal.

In the early 1830s the area now designated as Douglas was raw prairie where two old Indian trails, later to become Cottage Grove Avenue and Vincennes Avenue, joined together into a single route northward into Chicago. From the Wabash Valley to the southwest came cattle and wagons to travel the old Vincennes Road, while from the east settlers and traders made their way along old Lake Shore Road. Transportation through this area was made easier in 1850–51 when the Southern Plank Road was built by a private company which collected tolls from those who wanted to drive their vehicles in and out of Chicago. But this road lasted only a few years, for its

wooden planks, thrown down laterally across heavy beams, soon broke up under the weight of wagon traffic and were carried away to serve as firewood or fencing for local farmers.

As early as 1837 cattle drovers arriving in Chicago stopped at Myrick's Tavern, located at what is today Cottage Grove and 29th Street. Around the tavern were a few pens where cattle could be held until they were sold. In 1856 John B. Sherman, who eventually would organize the Union Stock Yard and Transit Company, bought the Myrick property and set up a stockyard. This served as one of the numerous marketing facilities which operated until the newer facility was established in 1865. Even before this consolidation, railroads were replacing the earlier cattle drives, but after the organization of the Union Stock Yard they became the chief means of transporting cattle into the Chicago area. As a result, the stockyards located in what is now Douglas were closed and residential development began in this area.

In 1852, Stephen A. Douglas, lawyer, politician, and land speculator, had purchased a 70-acre tract of land along the lake between 33rd and 35th. Douglas was

an inspired urban developer who wanted to attract well-to-do neighbors to his subdivision. In the Oakenwald Subdivision Map, which he recorded in 1855, Douglas designated three acres for specific purposes. One was a tract to be donated to an educational institution; two others, farther east, were marked as residential parks. These became the elegant enclaves of Groveland Park and Woodland Park.

Douglas followed through on his plans. In 1856 he took up residence at Oakenwald, at what is now 34 East 35th Street. Two years earlier he had offered a 10-acre tract to the Presbyterian Church as a site for an institution of learning. The Presbyterians declined the offer, but in 1856 the Baptists accepted and proceeded to establish the first University of Chicago, which opened its doors in 1860. This spurred some residential growth in the Groveland and Woodland Park area. Although the first University of Chicago closed in 1886 because of financial difficulties, it became the precursor of the present institution of that name in Hyde Park.

Another kind of institution brought further population to the Douglas area during the Civil War. In 1861, having determined to establish a military camp at Chicago, officials of the Northern Military District of Illinois chose a large open picnic ground west of the University of Chicago as the site. The specific bounds of Camp Douglas were 31st and 33rd, with Forest (Giles) on the west and Cottage Grove on the east. Before early 1862, about 30,000 members of various Illinois regiments were trained for battle at this camp. It then was made into a prisoner-of-war camp for Confederate soldiers. At the end of the Civil War all the buildings of the installation were torn down with the exception of the hospital which was taken over by the county. Throughout its existence, however, Camp Douglas sparked interest in the area around it, and new homeowners built homes near it.

During the 1870s and 1880s, the two private parks continued to attract residents, most of whom were American-born Protestants. Groveland Park was the more fashionable of the two and by 1880 provided sites for the homes of Joy Morton, founder of the Morton Salt Company; Judge James R. Doolittle, Jr.; Gustav Liljencrantz, engineer and city surveyor; and Elias Colbert, University of Chicago professor and commerce editor for the *Chicago Tribune*. Woodland Park developed more slowly but was completely settled during the 1880s. It included the residences of such Chicago personages as George H. Jones, owner of an iron works; M. S. Embree, owner of a South Side lumber company; and Norman B. Ream, a wealthy investor in city property. Groveland Park residents expressed their sense of exclusiveness by erecting an iron fence around their private park in 1897; Woodland Park residents followed suit a few years later.

From its earliest years the Douglas area was rich in transportation. Although many of the neighborhood residents were suffi-

ciently wealthy to commute to the Loop in their carriages, the Illinois Central Railroad, which stopped at 35th Street, provided an attractive alternative. In addition, the State Street horsecar line offered quick access from its southern terminal at 39th by the early 1860s. With the establishment of the Union Stock Yard in 1865, transportation boomed. The Cottage Grove horsecar line was extended south to 39th as were lines on Indiana and Wentworth. During the same period, the State Street line was extended south to Root, where it turned west to run into the Union Stock Yard. Cable car installation began on the South Side in 1881, and by 1883 the State Street Cable Line ran as far south as 55th. In 1894 the Indiana Street line was electrified, the first South Side line to receive the benefit of the new technology. Taken together, these lines formed a transportation access corridor which connected both the Loop and the stockyards with the Douglas community.

Such excellent transportation promoted quick residential development in Douglas. Large single family dwellings appeared along Dearborn, State, Wabash, Michigan, and Indiana in the 1880s. Even as these were being constructed, however, industrial employment outside the neighborhood was bringing pressure for working-class housing within it. Packingtown to the west, the railroad shops at 26th and Federal and at 39th and Stewart, and a number of breweries located north and northwest of the neighborhood, all brought working-class families to Douglas. The first visible response to their needs was the installation of some small balloon-frame houses and a few brick cottages along Federal Street. The presence of excellent transportation into the neighborhood also encouraged the construction of apartment houses. Around the

time of the World's Fair, these multiple unit buildings made their appearance around Groveland and Woodland parks. By 1900 Douglas was residentially mature.

During the last three decades of the nineteenth century, many different ethnic groups moved to and through Douglas. The Irish came first, mainly settling along Federal Street, although they were scattered throughout the neighborhood. Their presence was reflected in the organization of St. James's parish in 1855. The Irish and other Chicago Catholics also helped form another important Douglas institution, De La Salle Institute. This parochial academy was opened in 1892 at the northeast corner of 35th and Wabash, and at the time of its founding was close to an elegant street on which such prominent Catholic families as those of John and Michael Cudahy, the meat-packing moguls, had their residences. The school for young men was specifically located to take advantage of the neighborhood's transportation connections, including the South Side Elevated.

De La Salle quickly built a record of solid performance. The *Chicago Times Herald* of January 4, 1897, proclaimed that "in its six years of existence, it has earned for itself the reputation of being the leading educational institution for boys in the city." The school emphasized business education but its graduates distinguished themselves in other areas as well. Three of the city's political leaders, Mayors Martin Kennelly, Richard J. Daley, and Michael A. Bilandic graduated from De La Salle.

Soon after the Irish moved into the Douglas neighborhood some of the city's leading Jewish families settled there. In 1881 Michael Reese Hospital opened its doors at 29th and Cottage Grove Avenue. Although non-sectarian, the hospital was, in

Stephen A. Douglas Monument, 636 East 35th Street. Leonard Volk, whose artistic career was aided by Douglas, was commissioned to do this sculpture in the late 1860s but the Civil War and lack of money forced a twenty year delay. Eventually the State of Illinois put up $84,000 of the total cost of $90,000 and the work was completed in May 1881. Douglas's body was interred in a marble sarcophagus under the base of the statue. The monument was declared a national historic landmark on September 28, 1977. The tracks of the Illinois Central are at the right. Jevne & Almini lithograph, CHS.

a sense, an offshoot of an earlier medical facility built by the Jewish community on LaSalle in the Loop in 1867 but subsequently destroyed by the fire of 1871. Eight years later, Michael Reese (originally Ries)—a German Jewish immigrant who had made a fortune in real estate in California—died, leaving instructions that $200,000 of his legacy be used for charitable purposes. His heirs used the money to build a hospital bearing his name. The gift statement commanded that "sufferers, no matter of what religion or nationality, if found worthy and there be room, be admitted." By the turn of the century the hospital was straining to meet the demand for its services. Immediately after the Iroquois Theatre fire, the United Hebrew Charities raised $400,000 for a new hospital building which was ready for use in June 1907.

As its population increased, Douglas began to develop its own business center. By the 1890s stores could be found on 31st between State and Prairie, on State from 31st to 39th, on 35th from State to Cottage Grove, and on 39th extending east and west from State. The activities of the businessmen along these streets, especially those along Cottage Grove, show the changing character of the area between the 1890s and 1910. Following the World's Columbian Exposition in 1893, the Edison Company began to install street lights on the North Side. The company wanted to sell lights to South Siders as well and chose Cottage Grove Avenue between 22nd and 39th as a target area for its marketing effort. Through the efforts of the Edison group, thirty-nine businessmen along Cottage Grove signed up to try the new electric lights, and the company began installation of matched street lights on the avenue.

Out of this organizational effort of 1896 came the Cottage Grove Improvement Association. Once this group had obtained street lights it changed its name to the South Side Property Owners and Business Men's Association and promptly set out to secure neighborhood support for increased tax assessments for street paving. The effort was so successful that most of the streets and alleys in Douglas were soon paved. By 1900 the organization played a social role as well, holding dances and parties to supplement its civic activities. The latter were maintained at a high level throughout the early decades of the twentieth century. In 1906 the South Side Property Owners supported the installation of new sewerage treatment facilities for the area; in 1923 city-wide zoning; and in 1926 the filling in of Bubbly Creek and improvement of Pershing Road. After 1908, as residential property owners began to move out of the area, the organization once again changed its name and adjusted its purpose. Now called the South Side Business Men's Association it represented neighborhood business interests and put pressure on the city to maintain a high level of services along shopping streets.

As whites left Douglas blacks moved in. Some blacks had lived along Rhodes, Vernon, Calumet, and South Park (Dr. Martin Luther King, Jr. Drive) north and south of 26th Street from the 1870s onward. By 1900 they occupied a good portion of the houses west of State and south as far as 35th Street. The Great Migration of blacks from the South to Chicago prompted by World War I economic conditions led to an expansion of the South Side ghetto. Whereas in 1916 it had encompassed the west side of State from 29th to 35th, in the course of the next two years it extended southward to 47th and by the 1920s to 55th Street. During the next decade 35th and State became the equivalent of the Loop for Chicago's black community.

The role played by two institutions, a church and a community center, in Douglas during and after World War I, illustrates the texture of black life there in a period of expanding population. The Olivet Baptist Congregation had been founded by a number of black families in 1853. Its first meeting place was in the Loop but by 1893 the congregation was able to purchase three lots at 27th and Dearborn in Douglas on which a church was built. When the exigencies of World War I created a demand for labor in the Chicago area, blacks from less prosperous regions asked the Olivet congregation to help them migrate to Chicago and assist them after their arrival. The Olivet congregation responded by taking over a building across the street from the church and making it available for use by newly arrived blacks. The two upper stories were converted into a Working Men's Home and a relief dining room was set up downstairs.

The expansion of Olivet's activities increasingly led to overcrowding of the church facilities. An ideal opportunity presented itself when the white First Baptist Congregation at 31st Street and South Park decided to move to another location and offered its property for sale to the Olivet congregation. The latter bought the building and held its first service there in September 1918. During the race riot of the following year the congregation faced a severe test. It responded by becoming the headquarters of the Peace and Protective Association which for forty days attempted to bring calm to the riot-torn South Side while defending and assisting riot victims.

Another important institution for black

Olivet Baptist Church, southeast corner
of 31st Street and South Park Boulevard, 1962.
Chicago's First Baptist congregation
moved into this elegant edifice in 1876; Olivet
Baptist, a black congregation, purchased
the building during World War I. The Lake
Meadows apartments are behind the church.
Photo by Glenn E. Dahlby, CHS.

Aldine Square (top right), ca. 1900.
Located on Vincennes between 37th
and 39th, this residential park was developed
in 1876 by lawyer and builder Uzziel P. Smith.
By 1885 Aldine Square was completely
built up. The housing began to deteriorate during World War I. Renamed DeSaible Square
in 1936, the park was demolished after 1949 as
part of South Side urban renewal. CHS.

Michael Reese Hospital (lower right), northeast
corner of 29th and Ellis, 1918. Opened in
1907, this seven-story, 241-bed facility was
designed by architect Richard E. Schmidt. By
1955 the Reese complex had grown to 19
buildings. Photo gift of Rand McNally, CHS.

residents of Douglas was the Frederick Douglass Center organized in 1904 by Mrs. Celia Parker Woolley. This organization was created primarily to serve the blacks of the immediate neighborhood, but its activities affected many more of the 75,000 blacks who lived on the South Side. The purposes of the Center were to promote better race relations and to provide settlement house activities for the surrounding community. The latter services included instruction in domestic science and child care for women; the organization of boys' and girls' clubs; and finding jobs for those newly arrived in the city. The Douglass Center also handled cases of discrimination in employment and housing.

By 1920 Douglas had 58,388 residents, of whom 74 percent were black. A decade later that number was reduced to 50,285 with 89 percent of the total black. By the time of the 1940 census blacks made up 93.7 percent of the total neighborhood population of 53,124. That census also recorded 87.5 percent of all Douglas residents as renters, many living in converted single-family homes that had been built before 1900.

Even before the 1940 census was taken, the Chicago Housing Authority had made plans to use federal money to erect new housing in the Douglas community area. In 1941 the 1,658 unit Ida B. Wells Housing Project at 37th and South Parkway was opened for its first tenants. About 60 percent of this project is in Douglas; the remainder is in Oakland. The houses torn down to make way for the Wells project were primarily old brownstones and late Victorian single-family dwellings which had been converted into buildings of small units with kitchenettes. Nine years after the project was opened, another 800 units of

public housing were added in Douglas with the completion of the Dearborn Homes. This project, which stands at 27th and State, replaced an old slum of small cottages which had once housed railroad and stockyard workers.

By 1940 two private not-for-profit institutions in Douglas, the Illinois Institute of Technology and Michael Reese Hospital, were also considering redevelopment. The *Daily News* of April 10, 1958 summed up the situation when it noted, "Hemmed in by slums, the expanding institutions had to choose between these alternatives:—They could move their entire physical plants to new sites. —Or they could stay and build outward into the areas of decay. Their decision was based on a combination of courage and practicality. They stayed—and thereby created a nucleus for the whole [South Side] redevelopment program."

The Illinois Institute of Technology was the product of a merger between two institutions, one of which, the Armour Institute of Technology, had its origins in Douglas. Founded with money donated by Philip Armour of the meatpacking family, the institute which bore the family's name was built in 1891 on Federal Street between 32nd and 33rd. Meanwhile, Chicago businessman Allen C. Lewis, who died in 1877, had left behind a large estate for the founding of a technical school. This money established the Lewis Institute at Madison and Damen on the Near West Side in 1896.

In the 1930s both institutions were suffering from a lack of financial support and other resources needed to offer a technological education. They decided to merge in the hope that their combined means would enable the newly created school to forge forward. The old Armour Institute site became the nucleus for the expanded 100-

acre campus which stretched from 31st to 35th and from Michigan Avenue to the New York Central tracks.

Michael Reese Hospital and IIT both made a commitment to remain on the South Side prior to World War II, but the outbreak of hostilities postponed publication of any overall plan to stabilize the neighborhood. In 1946 the two institutions joined to found the South Side Planning Board which was charged with the task of drawing up a master plan for the rehabilitation of the whole area. This action by two major institutions represented a deliberate attempt to change the neighborhood's future.

In 1947 the State of Illinois passed an act establishing the Chicago Land Clearance Commission. This agency was authorized to reclaim and combine small parcels of land, write off the excess value, and sell large parcels back to institutions and private developers. The Federal Urban Renewal Act of 1949 provided money for the land clearance and urban redevelopment proposed by the South Side Planning Board. Such backing was necessary, for the South Side Plan developed by the two institutions designated an area of seven square miles for rehabilitation. Its boundaries were Cermak Road to the north, Lake Michigan to the east, 47th Street to the south, and the Pennsylvania Railroad to the west.

In part this institutional expansion called for the construction of housing. In 1946, as one indication of Michael Reese's commitment to remain in the area, board members had set up a corporation to build a set of high rises on the east side of King Drive between 26th and 31st. The 1,080 moderate income units were ready for occupancy by 1958. But even institutions the size of Michael Reese needed outside capital to solidify their renewal effort. Fortunately, the South Side Commission's plan was sufficiently attractive to induce the New York Life Insurance Company to finance the Lake Meadows high rise and shopping center developments on the east side of South Parkway between 31st and 35th streets. The first of the 2,000 apartments were completed in 1953, the last in 1968.

The New York Life project demonstrates the significance of the Land Clearance Commission's work. The Commission purchased the land for this project for $16 million and then sold it back to New York Life for $3.4 million. The insurance company's stated goal at the time that it began construction was to make 4 percent over a fifty-year period. As other investment opportunities presented themselves and interest rates rose, New York Life sold this complex to the real estate development and management firm of Draper and Kramer in 1969.

The efforts of the South Side Commission, demonstrated by the clearance and redevelopment of Michael Reese, IIT, Lake Meadows, and Prairie Shores, led Mercy Hospital to reevaluate its decision to move. Mercy Hospital had been located on the Near South Side since 1852 and thus had strong ties to the area. In the 1940s a debate arose as to whether the hospital should expand at its existing site or whether it should try to relocate. The controversy continued over the next fifteen years.

Meanwhile, as the Near South Side showed new life the Sisters of Mercy began a $9 million drive for new construction. The expanded Mercy Hospital complex, including a new 519-bed hospital was constructed between 1964 and 1968. The cost was $24 million, with another $6 million spent for support buildings. Thus, the Near South Side came to have yet another important institutional anchor.

These private redevelopment efforts were supported by further construction sponsored by the Chicago Housing Authority. In 1955 a 650-unit extension was added to the Ida B. Wells project completed fourteen years earlier. But the greatest building year for modern Douglas was 1958. Three hundred and twenty-six units were opened as the Prairie Avenue Courts located at 26th and Prairie, while the Stateway Gardens constructed at 35th and State contained 1,644 units. The latter project was a northern neighbor to the Robert Taylor Homes. The two projects ran from 35th to 54th Place, replacing the notorious Federal Street slum which had existed for half a century. Douglas received more public housing in the 1960s. About half of the Clarence Darrow project of 479 units opened in 1961 in the northeastern part of the community.

Redevelopment had a dramatic impact on the Douglas neighborhood. The first noticeable change was a decrease in population. In 1950 the population of Douglas had reached a decennial high of 78,745 persons, with 97.1 percent black. Two decades later, only 43,705 people resided in the neighborhood of whom 86.5 percent were black. However, this lower percentage of blacks did not mean that whites were scattered evenly through the community area. Instead, they were clustered together, primarily in the Lake Meadows–Prairie Shores complex.

Given the recent history of Douglas it is hardly surprising that most of the population lives in rental units. In 1950, 89.9 percent did so and by 1970 this had risen to 94.5 percent. But the units were turning over at a slower rate than during the previous decades. The 1960 census indicated that 81.9 percent of all families had lived in a different housing unit during the previous five years. The comparable figure for 1970 was only 55.4 percent.

In the 1880s Douglas had two distinct classes of inhabitants: lower-paid workers who lived west of State along the railroad tracks, and an enclave of wealthy homeowners who lived around Groveland and Woodland parks. In the 1970s this stratification, though less pronounced, still persists. The more prosperous inhabitants of Douglas today live in the Lake Meadows-Prairie Shores complex and the residential spillovers from Michael Reese, IIT, and Mercy Hospital. The inhabitants of the public housing projects suffer from underemployment rather than unemployment, and consequently have a much lower living standard than their neighbors in the privately financed housing. The fact that Douglas has three major institutions and a large number of public housing projects makes for a wide range of incomes in the area. In 1970, for example, 25.4 percent of family units reported incomes between $10,000 and $25,000. In the same year 24.9 percent of family units reported incomes below $5,000.

If the age of housing units is any indication of quality, then Douglas residents live better than they did thirty or forty years ago. Of the 17,010 housing units in the neighborhood, 64.4 percent were built as part of the thirty-year redevelopment effort that began in the late 1940s. Thus, what began as a suburban community of single-family homes in the 1850s, is now an area distinguished by the institutions which make their home there as well as by the rental unit housing which has become prevalent in the post-World War II period.

3344 South Wabash, 1910. This large brick single-family house stood on a 50-foot frontage in an elegant section of South Wabash. Built in the early 1880s, it was the home of the celebrated black prize fighter Jack Johnson at the time that this photograph was taken. *Daily News* photo, gift of Field Enterprises, CHS.

Northeast corner of 30th and Wabash, 1949. These multiple-family buildings were more than sixty years old when this photograph was taken. The original subdivider had intended that lots on this street be 50 feet wide, but the builder who erected the dwellings put three on two lots. Photo by Tedward A. Dumetz, Jr., CHS.

Old wooden tenements, north side of 37th Street between Ellis and Lake (now Lake Park Avenue), undated. These houses reportedly were built when Camp Douglas was being constructed. Their working-class character was apparent from the beginning and at some time in their history they picked up the appellation "Washer Woman's Row." CHS.

S. R. Crown Hall, Illinois Institute of Technology. IIT expanded from 5 buildings on 7 acres in 1940, to 50 buildings on 114 acres in 1964. Crown Hall, named for the co-founder and first president of Material Service Corporation, was designed by Mies van der Rohe and dedicated on April 30, 1956. CHS.

OAKLAND

The community area of Oakland is bounded on the east by Lake Michigan, on the north by 35th Street, and on the south by 43rd. Its western boundary is formed by Vincennes Avenue between 35th and Pershing, east on Pershing to Cottage Grove Avenue, then along Cottage Grove to 43rd. If the boundaries of this lakeshore community seem somewhat artificial it is because this has been a highly volatile section of the city in recent decades.

The first settlement in what became the Oakland community area was begun by Charles Cleaver, Chicago's "original soap-fat man and tallow chandler." For more than twenty years, beginning in the 1830s, Cleaver ran "a clearing house for lard." Its location in 1850 was at Canal near Madison, on the west bank of the Chicago River. Then in 1851, as the central area of the city became more built up, Cleaver moved his oil factory to a new location on a swampy section of the Lake Michigan shoreline near the foot of 38th. The siting of this new plant gave the Cleaver operation a distinct locational advantage: it was only about a mile southeast of the Sherman Stock Yard which had begun in 1837 as Myrick's Stock Yard and Tavern, and about half a mile from the

more recently developed Cottage Grove Stock Yard which adjoined the Sherman facility.

Anticipating the efforts of George M. Pullman two decades later, Cleaver attempted to establish a company town around his factory by erecting a number of wooden cottages for his employees. Indeed, in one year alone he spent $60,000 for that purpose. In 1854 Cleaver added a small meeting house which was used as a school for the workers' children during the week and as a church on Sundays. Cleaver paid the minister who, by 1857, had enough communicants to organize the Oakland Congregational Church. The congregation used the hall as its first building. In 1866–67 Cleaver built Cleaver Hall, a second meeting place which served as a town hall and community entertainment center until it was finally torn down in 1886 because it was unsafe.

Cleaver took three other steps to develop his settlement. First, to insure connections with the central business district, he made an agreement with the Illinois Central Railroad Company whereby it agreed to have its trains stop at the Oakland Station, located on the north side of Oakwood Street where it intersected with the tracks. Cleaver

had to pay a $3,800 annual fee to cover the operating losses of the company until sufficient traffic developed. Second, Cleaver established a grocery and general store which was managed by his brother. This establishment was located at the intersection of Pier (38th) and Lake (Lake Park) Avenue and operated without competition for at least ten years. Third, while maintaining an office on South Water Street, Cleaver in 1857 moved into a new house named Oakwood Hall sited on a large lot at what is now 3938 South Ellis, or the northwest corner of Oakwood and Ellis. Finally, in October 1858, Cleaver opened a subdivision which included all the territory between Egan or 39th on the north, Maple or 41st on the south, Lake Michigan on the east, and Cottage Grove Avenue on the west. The area was now available for lot-by-lot development.

The part of the future neighborhood north of the Cleaverville settlement—the area between 35th and 38th from Vincennes to the lake—remained open during the 1850s while Charles Cleaver was organizing his little fiefdom. A remnant of the area's earlier days, Ellis Park is the centerpiece of the northern half of Oakland. Samuel Ellis, after whom the park and the avenue are named, ran a tavern, the Ellis Inn, at what is now the southwest corner of Lake (Lake Park) Avenue and 35th. It was ideally located to serve travelers entering Chicago, being near the intersection of the Vincennes Trail from the southwest and Lake Shore Road from the southeast. In 1851, Ellis had sold Charles Cleaver 22 acres of land. That land and an additional 72 acres formed the acreage for Cleaver's little development.

In locating his subdivision Cleaver was anticipating that the natural growth of Chicago would create a demand for his lots. When the city incorporated in 1837, its southern boundary was 22nd. The annexation of 1853 carried that boundary to 31st. The Town of Hyde Park was incorporated in 1861, with a northern boundary at Egan (Pershing). Thus Cleaverville, except for its northeastern corner, became part of Hyde Park. When Chicago annexed more territory to the south in 1863, it took in this little piece of Cleaverville, and the future neighborhood of Oakland became part of two different incorporated political units.

Charles Cleaver's promotional tactics brought population to Cleaverville in the 1850s. During the following decade other growth forces attracted new residents. The operation of Camp Douglas between 1861 and 1865, initially as a training ground for the Northern Illinois Militia and then as a camp for Confederate soldiers who had become prisoners of war, brought attention to the whole area surrounding the camp grounds, located between 31st and 33rd and Cottage Grove and Forest (Giles). Then, in 1867, Cleaverville's access to the city was improved with the extension of the Cottage Grove horsecar line to 39th Street. These developments inspired new interest in the Cleaverville settlement and led real

estate promoters to resubdivide the little community in 1871, renaming it Oakland. The boundaries of this development were the Union Stock Yards Railway which paralleled 41st on the south, the city limits between Hyde Park and Chicago or an eastern extension of 39th on the north, Cottage Grove on the west, and the lake on the east.

During the late 1860s and early 1870s, Oakland became an "attractive little suburb," and a "stopping place for both city and suburban residents." The residences constructed during this period resembled Cleaver's fine house rather than his workers' cottages. By 1874 Oakland could claim a number of families who were part of Chicago's social elite. These included Senator Lyman Trumbull and his brother, Illinois Central attorney, George Trumbull; real estate dealer George G. Pope; lawyer and fertilizer manufacturer Joseph F. Bonfield; grocer Samuel Faulkner; paper bag manufacturer Lucius G. Fisher; and Albion R. and George H. Miller, who were partners in a wholesale cutlery and hardware business.

While the panic of 1873 retarded Oakland's growth, the area recovered quickly. By 1876 several hundred people resided in the community and population increased rapidly after 1881, when a steam dummy-powered railroad connected Hyde Park with the 39th Street terminal of the Cottage Grove horsecar line. The following year that line was mechanized with cable, decreasing commuting time between Oakland and the Loop.

The presence of the cable line terminal at 39th made the Cottage Grove–39th Street intersection, quickly dubbed the "five crossings" by locals, a significant retail center. Clarke and Tingey's grocery was especially important for it also served as the Oakland Post Office. The Hyde Park anti-saloon laws

were yet another reason for the development of the five crossings. Hyde Park residents had voted themselves into a dry district under the state's local option laws, with the result that there were no saloons in the area except at a few business intersections where old drinking establishments were allowed to remain as a controlled public service. Residents in the northern half of Hyde Park therefore found the five crossings saloons, located on the Chicago side of the 39th Street boundary, a pleasant incentive for transacting their other retail business at that location. One instance is recorded of a building that straddled the Chicago–Hyde Park dividing line: the southern or Hyde Park half served as a pool hall, while the northern or Chicago half was a saloon. Years later Oakland residents recalled that this pool hall had a particularly large and devoted group of patrons.

In 1853 the Oakland School District census recorded a population of 3,012 persons residing in the suburb. Of these, only six were unable to read and write English, and the census made special note of the fact that even these six were literate in their own languages. Oakland also had its share of churches. The Oakland Congregational Church, founded with the encouragement of Charles Cleaver, eventually became, after several reorganizations and some years of controversy, the Memorial Congregational Church, located at 40th and Drexel. The Memorial Baptist Church, located at 35th and Rhodes after 1871, traced its lineage back to the Edina Baptist Congregation at Harrison and Edina Place (now Plymouth Court). Catholics organized the Church of the Holy Angels in 1880. It was sited on the south side of Oakwood Boulevard near Langley Avenue. Meanwhile, on the corner of 41st and Prairie stood the Forty-First

Myrick House and the stockyards, 29th and Cottage Grove Avenue. This sketch of one of the predecessors of the Union Stock Yard was done by an unknown artist. CHS.

Oakwood Boulevard west from Drexel Boulevard, 1892. Sculpted plantings installed by the South Park Commission contributed to the elegant character of this wide intersection. At the right is the Allen Apartments, a posh flat building that later became the DuSable Hotel. To the left are the steeples of the Memorial Baptist Church and the All Souls Unitarian Church. Gravure from *Chicago, 1893*, CHS.

Northwest corner of 41st and Cottage Grove Avenue, 1967. Although this corner developed as part of a commercial section in the 1880s, this combined four-story apartment and commercial structure was erected in the next decade, replacing several small wooden stores. Located only one-half block from the Stock Yards Railroad, which also held the elevated line that served the Yards after 1903, this continued to be a fashionable residential building until World War I. Photo by Sigmund J. Osty, CHS.

3305–3307 Rhodes Avenue, 1950. These two houses were an anachronism in the 1890s when they were the only wooden, single-family residences on a block of brick and stone-fronted apartment buildings. When this photograph was taken, the houses were occupied by blacks, one of whom made his living by delivering coal and ice and selling snacks to South Side residents. Photo by Tedward A. Dumetz, Jr., CHS.

Street Presbyterian Church which had been organized as a congregation through the efforts of the Presbyterian League in 1870.

Other kinds of organizations indicated the presence of those who had the time and money for recreational activity. Because the area was so heavily Republican in the 1880s, a group of residents financed the construction every four years of the Republican Wigwam, a small building in which they gathered for their political activities. After 1892, when Democrats became more numerous in the community, the custom of building a Wigwam for each national election ended, but the Republicans continued to hold their political meetings in an armory at the northeast corner of Oakwood and Ellis. This armory was erected in 1889 by the Oakland Rifles, a political marching club organized two years earlier, but many other groups also used this armory for their meetings. After the turn of the century it was removed to the corner of 39th and Langley where it became first a dancing school and then a roller skating rink. So prolific was the club life of Oakland that the activities of the residents spilled into neighboring Kenwood. The Oakland Club, for example, had a cottage on Marshall Field's property at the corner of 46th and Grand Boulevard.

In 1889 Hyde Park, including the suburb of Oakland, was annexed to Chicago. In the decade before annexation, most of the population of the community was "American," but store signs in the five crossings shopping district indicated the presence both of Germans and of German Jews. During the 1890s the Irish arrived. Many of these families were upwardly mobile residents moving eastward from the stockyards neighborhoods. Continuing population pressure placed a high demand on living space, and by 1895 Oakland was residentially mature.

Maturity did not mean stability, however. Between 1895 and 1910, many of Oakland's wealthier residents began to leave. Meanwhile, Loop workers, who found the neighborhood's excellent transportation and shopping facilities particularly convenient, entered from the north. To meet the constantly escalating demand for housing, new owners began to convert some of the neighborhood's old large houses into apartments. The neighborhood, therefore, was in transition before the arrival of a significant number of black families. But racial change soon became part of the transition process.

The transition was hastened by the new kinds of housing erected in the 1890s and the 1910s. Just before the turn of the century, mass-built, single-family dwellings appeared. Neighborhood residents were appalled at their cheap appearance but seemed unable to resist when a contractor named Berkeley obtained the right to widen the alley which ran between Ellis and Lake Park between 41st and 45th. The builder then opened Berkeley Street and, along both sides, built "row on row of queer little houses with the windows cut into corners of the house and weird looking façades in front," as an old resident described them in the 1920s. "He knew only one plan for a house, and they were all turned out of the same mold like a pan of biscuits; one could find dozens of houses that he built scattered throughout the community."*

The other significant development was the beginning of construction of multiple-unit buildings. Before 1910 apartments had been created by conversion. During the next decade apartment houses began to replace single-family dwellings. This construction coincided with the installation of the Kenwood Elevated Line, which entered the neighborhood on right-of-way secured from

the Chicago Junction Railway and linked the stockyards with Oakland. At first the new apartment units housed people who took some interest in the community, but between 1918 and 1925, long-term residents became aware that the apartments were attracting persons who were "mobile, with very few connections within the community." Together, the construction of the elevated and the apartment house boom led to a dramatic downturn in the quality of the neighborhood.

Between 1900 and 1910 blacks began to enter the community, pushing southward from their cramped quarters in the neighborhoods of the Near South Side and Douglas and eastward from the State Street black belt. In the 1910s this movement was confined north of 39th, along Vincennes, Vernon, and Rhodes avenues. In 1920 there were 16,540 residents in Oakland, of whom 17 percent were black. During the next decade the core of Oakland—between Oakwood Boulevard and 43rd, and from Vincennes to the lake—remained white, except for Oakwood Boulevard and its immediate side streets. In 1930 Germans, English, Irish, and Canadians were the chief foreign stock, while a small Japanese American community had developed between 35th and 39th on Lake Park. By now, 28.9 percent of the population was black. Overall, Oakland's population had declined to 14,962 by 1930.

The change in the neighborhood was mirrored in the institution known as Lincoln Center. In 1883, the Reverend Jenken Lloyd Jones, pastor of All Souls Church, an independent congregation which had broken away from the Unitarians, started the institution. Lincoln Center was not a social settlement but rather a community center, and its programs were mainly intellectual rather than recreational. Jones's hope was that the institution would function as "a sort of Hague for the settlement of religious and racial differences." A center building was constructed in 1895. From its opening and because of its purpose, blacks were invited to participate in the center's activities, which included the first University of Chicago extension lectures. But integration created a problem, for as more blacks became involved in the center's activities whites withdrew from them. By the mid-1920s more than half of the children and two-thirds of the adults who were regular participants in the institution's activities were black.

Oakland fell on hard times during the Great Depression. Two significant changes occurred. The first was a further decline in population down to 14,500. The second was that the proportion of blacks in the Oakland population fell: in 1940 only 22.1 percent of the total population was black, compared to 28.9 percent a decade earlier. The explanation for this shift is to be found in two population movements. The first was an influx of Southern whites, who entered what had become a rooming house district west of Cottage Grove Avenue. The second appears to have been continued movement of white stockyard workers into Oakland, where rents were low enough to allow a quick way out of the low quality housing to be found around Packingtown.

In the 1940s, however, the black ghetto to the north exploded into Oakland. Population rose 68.7 percent to reach 24,464, with blacks constituting 77.4 percent of the total. The racial change continued in the following decade. Of the 24,378 people in Oakland in 1960, blacks made up 98.2 percent. Almost all of this increase occurred through conversion of older units into small apartments and kitchenettes. The only new units constructed came through public housing. Some 40 percent of the 1,652-unit Ida B. Wells Homes completed in 1941 were in Oakland. In 1953, the 150-unit Victor A. Olander Homes was opened, and three years later a 150-unit extension was added to it. The other public housing erected was the Madden Park project at Pershing Road and Ellis. About two-thirds of this project lies in Oakland. Thus, in 1960, 13 percent of the housing stock in the community was new. The remainder consisted primarily of overcrowded slums, with 87.6 percent of all units occupied by renters.

The mighty impact of the federally financed demolition ball became apparent the next decade. By 1970 the population of Oakland had dropped to 18,291, 98.9 percent being black. Further demolitions since 1970 have led to a further drop in population.

The future prospects of this neighborhood area remain uncertain. Its rich transportation resources make redevelopment possible, but community representatives speaking in 1971 and again in 1977 were skeptical and expressed their fear that redevelopment would follow the pattern laid out in Hyde Park, where poor blacks had to be relocated because they could not afford the new units being constructed. In spite of efforts at community organization, Oakland residents remain doubtful about their ability to control the fate of their neighborhood in the years to come.

---

* Document #7 in Vivien M. Palmer's *Social Backgrounds of Chicago's Local Communities* (1930).

Announcement for a meeting of the Oakland-Kenwood Property Owners' Association, 1941. Neighborhood citizens formed a property owners' association, then a planning association, when the neighborhood experienced rapid racial and economic change. The groups lobbied for more policemen, for control of drug-related juvenile crime, for better neighborhood services, and against "sneak conversions" and "zoning violations" that "threaten slums for Oakland-Kenwood." CHS.

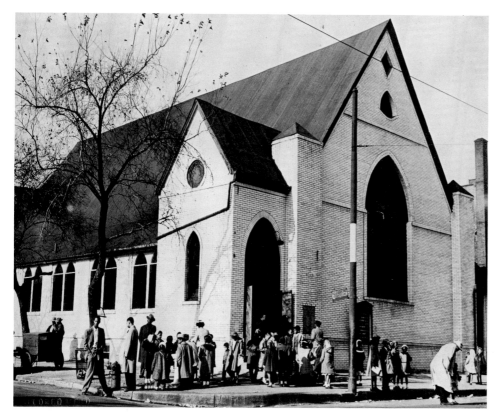

West Point Baptist Church, 3572 Cottage Grove Avenue, 1954. Organized by a group of 85 Mississippians in 1917, the West Point congregation purchased the old St. Mark's Episcopal Church located at 36th and Cottage Grove in 1918. In 1970, the congregation of 3,000 dedicated a new church adjacent to this building, which was remodeled into an educational center. Photo by Mildred Mead, CHS.

South Side Bank and Trust Company, northeast corner, 47th and Cottage Grove Avenue, September 1952. The South Side State Bank opened its doors at 4301 Cottage Grove in Oakland in 1919, then moved to this location in the early 1920s. A new group of owners purchased the bank in 1972 and moved it to 6104 North Northwest Highway, giving it the name of the Bank of Commerce and Industry. A second South Side Bank now occupies the 47th and Cottage Grove Avenue site. Photo by J. Sherwin Murphy, CHS.

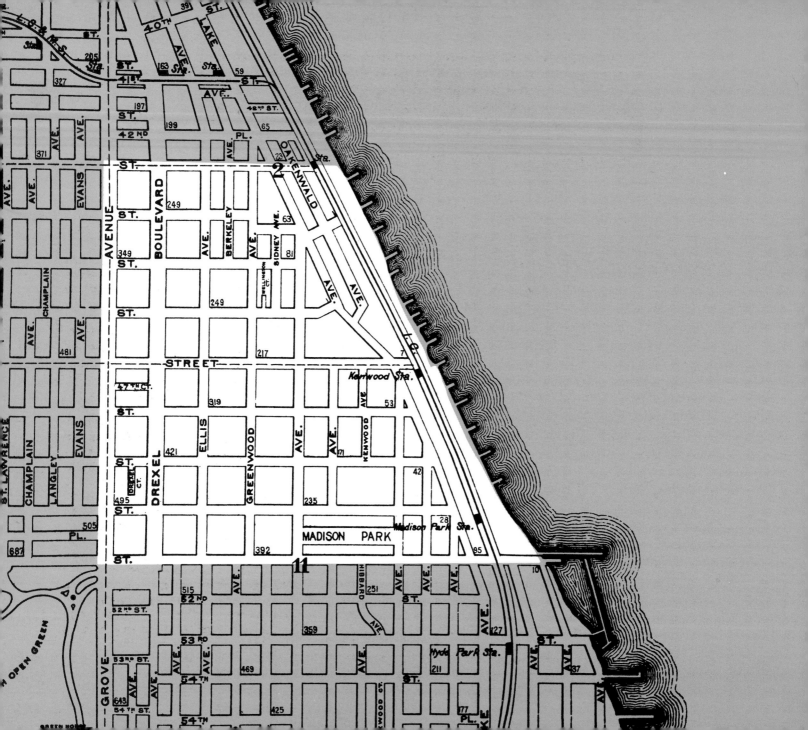

KENWOOD

The area known as Kenwood is bordered on the east by Lake Michigan, on the west by Cottage Grove Avenue, on the north by 43rd Street, and on the south by Hyde Park Boulevard (51st). As is the case with all Chicago neighborhoods, its boundaries have shifted in the course of its normal development.

Kenwood traces its origins back to 1856, when Dr. John A. Kennicott, a dentist, believing that Chicago was becoming too "citified," resolved to move to the country. He purchased an eight-acre estate: three acres surrounded the family house which was located south of 43rd Street near the Illinois Central tracks, and the remaining five lay between Greenwood and Woodlawn, north of 47th Street. Once established in his new home, Kennicott continued to practice dentistry in the city while enjoying the life of a gentleman farmer. He called his retreat Kenwood after his mother's family estate in Scotland.

Over the next three years a few other wealthy families moved in nearby, notably William Waters and John Remmer, executives of the Illinois Central; Pennoyer Levi Sherman, a well-known Loop attorney; and Dr. William B. Egan, a wealthy capitalist, who built "Egandale," a palatial house surrounded by grounds that extended along the south side of 47th from Woodlawn to Cottage Grove as far as 55th Street. Catering to this cluster of families, the Illinois Central in 1859 agreed to stop trains at 47th Street. When General George B. McClellan, then vice-president of the Illinois Central, opened the 47th Street station, he called it Kenwood and the name then spread to encompass the surrounding community.

By 1875 the houses and elegant grounds of Kenwood were one of Chicago's most attractive sights. A contemporary writer exclaimed: "If it were not invidious to draw a distinction between the many prosperous suburban towns of Hyde Park [Township], it might perhaps be in order to say that the suburb known as Kenwood was decidedly the most aristocratic of all—Kenwood is the Lake Forest of the South Side." The accolade was deserved, for in the decade before Prairie Avenue assumed preeminence on the South Side, Kenwood contained the homes of such notables as Norman P. Judd, a prominent lawyer who became a state senator; W. K. Akerman, treasurer of the Illinois Central; C. M. Cady, mayor of the town of Hyde Park; W. W. Hitchcock and C. B. Dupree, law partners in a prestigious Loop firm; Judge Van Hollis Higgins; Colonel George R. Clarke; and William H. Rand, founder of Rand, McNally & Company.

Improved transportation aided the growth of the suburban enclave. Between 1870 and 1878, a horsecar line was installed on Cottage Grove Avenue, connecting the 39th Street terminal of the State Street line with 55th. The construction of the South Parks system* also was important, since the eastern boundary of Washington Park formed the western boundary of the small community. The sons of the Philadelphia banker, Francis A. Drexel, made good use of the South Parks system when they deeded Drexel Boulevard to the South Park Commissioners and erected a statue honoring their father at the corner of Drexel and 51st. Their lots, lining both sides of the wide street, were quickly purchased by wealthy Chicagoans who built large mansions along the boulevard, adding to Kenwood's aristocratic character. Drexel Boulevard formed the eastern edge of an enclave of large single-family homes that extended east to

_____

*   See page 74.

Blackstone, between 43rd and 47th streets. By 1880 Kenwood had institutions appropriate to its status as the "crème de la crème of hamlets." It contained not only a brick public schoolhouse, but a female seminary run by Mrs. Kennicott, St. Paul's Episcopal Church at 4945 Dorchester, and a Congregational Church on 47th.

Many Kenwood residents opposed Chicago's 1889 annexation of Hyde Park,* of which they were a part. It was a "disastrous day when Hyde Park voted itself a part of Chicago, so selling its birthright," a former Kenwood resident recalled in 1940. Over the next two decades, Kenwood gradually lost its exclusive character as single-family home construction declined, and apartment houses began to appear along Drexel Boulevard and on Woodlawn, Dorchester, and Blackstone. A transportation improvement stimulated further change. The Kenwood branch of the South Side elevated was extended eastward to a terminal located at 42nd and the lake. Between 43rd and 47th Street, the effect was seen quickly. Owners converted old houses and large apartments into smaller efficiency units to meet the demand of Loop workers who commuted via the new transportation connection. By 1910, 47th Street had become a dividing line bisecting the Kenwood community, with the blocks to the south still holding their essential upper-class character. During the next decade, however, conversions to efficiency units, especially along the western streets of the southern section, accelerated. As a result, population density and overcrowding began to increase. What had been an exclusive suburban enclave in 1880 had become an urban neighborhood with a population of 21,068 by 1920.

From its annexation in 1889 through the 1920s, Kenwood remained sufficiently fashionable to attract representatives of the city's economic and political elite. These included architect Louis Sullivan; John G. Shedd, who headed Marshall Field & Company and donated the Shedd Aquarium to the city; Edward H. Kelly, mayor of the city; and Julius Rosenwald, who made his fortune with Sears, Roebuck, and Co. but is best remembered for his philanthropic activities. The backgrounds of these prominent residents of Kenwood varied. Kelly, for example, came from an Irish family in Bridgeport; Rosenwald represented the large number of Germans, especially German Jews, who made their way to Kenwood from neighborhoods farther north through the late nineteenth and early twentieth century. The English influence was seen in the establishment of private schools, including the Faulkner and Harvard schools for boys and the Starrett School for girls.

During the 1920s and 1930s Kenwood grew modestly. The population of the community area increased by 28 percent to reach 26,942 in 1930. Less than one percent of this total was black. Through the twenties, the most significant housing development was the construction of several new high-rise apartment buildings at the southeastern corner of the community east of the Illinois Central tracks. During the depression decade this new construction encouraged a further increase in population. By 1940 the community had 29,611 inhabitants, a rise of 9.9 percent in ten years. German Jews, the Irish, and the English continued to predominate among the foreign born, while the number of blacks increased only slightly.

World War II brought dramatic population shifts as a city-wide housing shortage led to severe overcrowding in many areas of Chicago. Kenwood was one of these: between 1940 and 1950 its population jumped by 20.6 percent to reach 35,705, and by the latter date 84.7 percent of the population was black. These trends continued over the next decade as population rose to 41,533 in 1960 with 83.9 percent being black.

The core of the white middle-class families who continued to live in Kenwood in the 1960s clustered in the large mansions situated between 48th and 51st Street and in the high-rise apartments west of the Illinois Central Railroad. University of Chicago students, most of whom were white, also resided in the community along the north side of Hyde Park Boulevard and in Madison Park, a private park laid out by William M. Dunham in 1869 as part of a small subdivision.

In 1930 there were just slightly over 8,000 dwelling units in Kenwood; thirty years later there were 15,428. But only 6 percent of this number had been erected after 1940, and 60 percent of the total units were in buildings that contained 10 or more flats, kitchenettes, and small apartments. Although planning for urban renewal in Hyde Park-Kenwood had begun in 1949, demolition by the Chicago Land Clearance Authority did not begin in Kenwood until shortly after the 1960 census was taken. Two years later, the Chicago Dwellings Association, a not-for-profit corporation that worked closely with the Chicago Housing Authority, broke ground for its first project in the community, a 9-story high-rise at 51st and Cottage Grove which was designated for elderly, middle-income families.

Meanwhile, there was great pressure to build new low-income housing in Kenwood to replace what was being demolished. But the planners who were involved in the Hyde Park-Kenwood Community Conference,* a

---

*   See page 80.

Residences of the Marvin A. Farr and Thaddeus Dean families at 4737 and 4747 South Woodlawn in Kenwood, 1889. Farr was a partner in the Loop real estate firm of James B. Goodman & Co., and Dean was president of the City Lumber Company located on the North Side. Both families moved into these residences in 1886. From *Picturesque Kenwood*, ca. 1889, CHS.

Greenwood Avenue School class picture, ca. 1886. This school became a part of the Chicago school system with the annexation of Hyde Park Township in 1889. Located at 1119 East 46th Street, it was renamed the Shakespeare School in 1904. Photo gift of Mrs. John Paul Welling, CHS.

grass roots organization fighting the spread of blight in the area, and those representing the South East Planning Commission, which essentially reflected the views of the University of Chicago, disagreed on what should be done. The Community Conference, in which various churches and social organizations were strongly represented, pressed for a community that was socio-economically as well as racially integrated. The South East Planning Commission and private developers, however, argued that the construction of public housing for low income groups along or near 47th Street would overshadow their efforts to maintain racial integration south of that street.

This debate became particularly bitter in 1964 when the Kenwood Town Homes Company was selected by the city to construct a 193-unit town house and duplex development between 47th and 48th, bordered by Ellis and Lake Park. Testifying on behalf of the project at a public hearing in 1964, Richard L. Mandel, attorney for the Kenwood Town Homes Company, stated the developer's position succinctly. "We set out to plan predominantly moderate cost houses of excellent design, and excellent site planning," he stated. "We think we have achieved this goal."

But private sector capital could not be found for Kenwood redevelopment until assurances had been given that the area to the north was not going to be rebuilt for the poor. The project was delayed four years. At that point approval was given for a 20-acre development along the south side of 47th between Ellis and Lake Park Avenue, then extending south along Lake Park past 49th Street. One 38-story and two 34-story high-rises were erected on that site, financed by the Amalgamated Clothing Workers of America. The Lake Village Corporation, a group of Chicago developers, meanwhile financed construction of 150 town houses to the west of the high-rises. Taken together these two projects have offered popular housing opportunities for those with moderate incomes. But at a social cost. In the course of demolition, many structures housing small businesses were removed and numerous poor families, mostly black, were forced to move to make redevelopment possible.

The 1970 census provided a dramatic demonstration of the remarkable changes wrought in Kenwood by a decade of renewal efforts. The total population had dropped to 26,987—a reduction of 35.0 percent. The south half of Kenwood had regained much of its former eminence. Although Kenwood is still far from being the elite suburb it was in the 1880s, the concern and efforts of its residents have restored the quality of living conditions there to a degree that few Chicagoans would have believed possible in the 1940s.

Winter scene near 42nd and Drexel, probably 1892. A wooden toboggan slide and an ice skating rink allowed residents along Grand Boulevard to have some winter fun at the time of the Columbian Exposition. Photo by J. W. Taylor, CHS.

Kehilath Anshe Mayriv Temple, 930 E. 50th Street, April 1952. The oldest Jewish congregation in Chicago, K.A.M. was organized in 1847. The temple in the photograph was completed in 1923 to serve the Hyde Park-Kenwood community. It was sold to Operation Push, the black civil rights organization, after K.A.M. merged with Temple Isaiah Israel at 1100 E. Hyde Park Boulevard in 1971. Photo by J. Sherwin Murphy, CHS.

Stock Yard and Kenwood branches of the South Side Elevated, 1957. Entrepreneur Frederick H. Prince spent $3,300,000 of his own money to build these lines so that workers in the yards and the Central Manufacturing District would have access to the neighborhoods to the east. In 1918 the Stock Yard "L" carried 21,000 passengers daily but during the 1940s and 1950s traffic declined and in 1957 this service was stopped. The structure was torn down the following year. Photo by John McCarthy, CHS.

West on 47th across Lake Park Avenue, July 1960. Urban renewal demolition had not yet begun when this photo of the eastern end of the black business district along 47th Street was taken. While a few of the sagging commercial structures remain standing on the north side of 47th, the buildings on the south side have been torn down to make way for Lake Village, a town house and garden apartment project completed in 1971 and for a 26-story apartment building financed by the Amalgamated Clothing Workers of America. Photo by J. Sherwin Murphy, CHS.

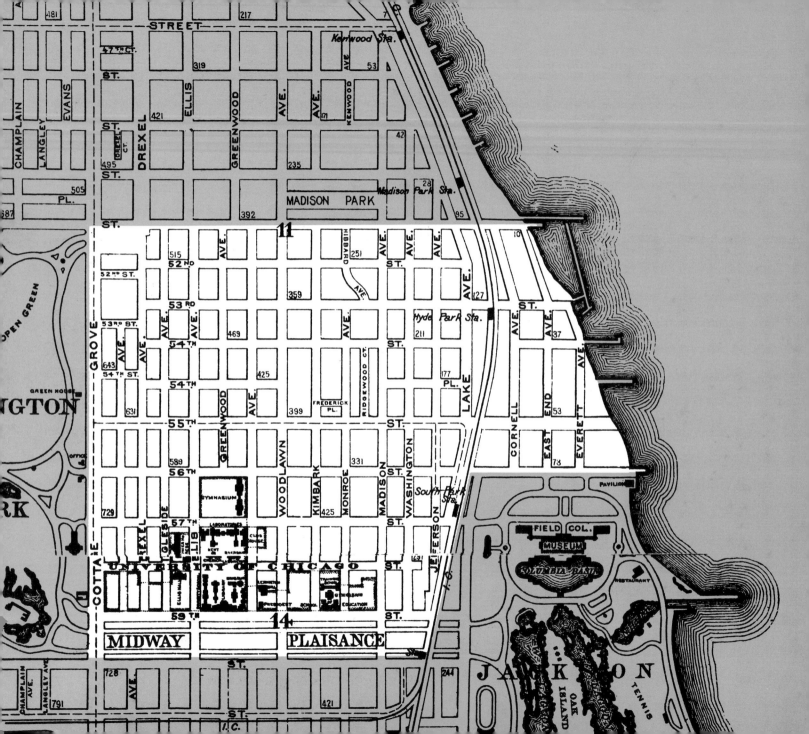

HYDE PARK

The present neighborhood of Hyde Park has passed through four distinct stages. It was established in the 1850s as an elite suburb attached to the city by the Illinois Central Railroad. In the early 1860s Hyde Park, together with other suburban settlements east of State Street, was split away from the Town of Lake to form Hyde Park Township. In the late 1880s, Hyde Park Township was annexed to the city of Chicago. In the early 1890s, the World's Columbian Exposition was held in Jackson Park, the construction of the fair coinciding with the erection of the first buildings of the University of Chicago along the Midway Plaisance. Occurring so closely together, these three events accelerated tendencies already apparent in the community during the first half of the 1880s, so that annexation notwithstanding, Hyde Park would continue to maintain a distinctive character. Finally, in the post-World War II era, Hyde Park would attract national attention as the University of Chicago and neighborhood residents joined in a fervent effort to combat the conditions which had led to the decline of many other South Side neighborhoods.

Considering its exciting history, Hyde Park had inauspicious beginnings. Within the present boundaries of the neighborhood—Lake Michigan on the east, Cottage Grove Avenue on the west, Hyde Park Boulevard on the north, and 60th Street on the south—real estate activity was dull during the 1830s and 1840s. At least one farmer, Obadiah Hooper, claimed a homestead within this area when the federal government opened the land around Chicago for settlement but was unable to maintain his right to the tract and lost it when it was sold for taxes. One resident who was successful for a time was Nathan Watson. By 1836 he had erected a small log cabin at the eastern end of what is now 53rd Street and had turned it into a tavern serving those who entered and left Chicago along the Lake Michigan beach trail.

It was Paul Cornell who transformed Hyde Park from its quiescent rural state into a bustling suburban settlement. The twenty-five-year old Cornell came west in May 1847, bringing with him a New York law degree, no significant amount of capital, large hopes, and a packet of business cards bearing the imprint *Paul Cornell, Attorney-at-Law, Chicago*. Over the next decade he worked in various Chicago law firms, first as a clerk, then as a trial lawyer, and finally as a collector of accounts for Eastern capitalists who had large holdings in the lakeside city. While employed by the law firm of Skinner and Hoyne, he met Stephen A. Douglas, who was promoting the Calumet region as an alternate industrial center to Chicago. Douglas was enthusiastic about real estate investment opportunities along the entire south shore and at one point remarked to Cornell, "Whenever you have a spare dollar, plant it between here (Chicago) and the Calumet. There the future city will lie."

Cornell had accumulated sufficient capital by 1852 to follow Douglas's advice. In that year he paid for a survey of a large tract of land along the southern lake shore. The following year he purchased 300 acres there and laid plans for developing the suburban town of Hyde Park. The choice of name was significant. While he admitted to a reporter in 1900 that he did not know which influenced his thinking more—Hyde Park in London or Hyde Park on the banks of the Hudson in the state of New York—he chose this name, associated with all that is elegant and gracious in living, for the sandy, swampy site for which he had such high hopes.

In 1856 Cornell began selling lots in what became the first Hyde Park subdivision, the area bounded by 51st, 55th, Dorchester, and the lake. Since the site had no particular amenities besides the lakefront, Cornell added them.

First, he sold 60 acres of land at the southern edge of his original Hyde Park development to the Illinois Central Railroad which bisected his property. By putting the railroad into the land development business and giving it a stake in the town's growth, he persuaded the company to stop six trains a day at 53rd Street, the location of the original Hyde Park station. Second, Cornell built a large hotel at 53rd Street near the lake as a rustic retreat for Chicagoans who wanted to get away from the hectic life of the city for a few days. It was also a place where families hunting for house lots could stay for a day or two while they explored the advantages of settling in Hyde Park or supervised the construction of their new homes.

Third, Cornell designated a portion of the lakefront which lay between 51st and 53rd east of East End Avenue (later Hyde Park Boulevard) as a "common." Finally, he undertook extensive negotiations with the Presbyterian Church, offering a four-square-block parcel on the lakefront south of the little park as a site for the Presbyterian Theological Seminary of the Northwest. When the Presbyterians decided to build on the North Side instead, Cornell lost the institutional anchor he badly wanted to help set a certain tone for the neighborhood, much as the first University of Chicago had done for Stephen A. Douglas's suburban settlement to the north. When the negotiations came to nothing Cornell opened these grounds for house lots.

During the first decade of its existence Hyde Park grew slowly, but those who moved there created the ambience Cornell aspired to. His relatives and business associates were numerous among the early purchasers of Hyde Park land. Some simply wanted large house lots, which in the first plan were laid out only 18 to the block, providing each owner with a minimum 50-foot frontage. Others, however, bought acreage contiguous to or near Cornell's original subdivision with the intention of opening their own suburban tracts for settlement when the time was ripe.

Hyde Park was only one of a number of small suburban settlements opened in the 1850s south of 39th Street (then the city limits) and east of State Street. The people who lived in these little enclaves quickly grew dissatisfied with the quality of the local government that they could obtain from the township of Lake, of which they were a part. Consequently, in 1861, the leaders of these small communities joined together in a successful petition to the Illinois General Assembly for the creation of a separate township of Hyde Park. This would include the original subdivision as part of a 48-square-mile area between 39th Street on the north, State Street on the west, and Lake Michigan on the east. At the time of its creation, the township of Hyde Park had 350 residents. Today urban planners would regard such action as a move in the direction of political balkanization. At the time it was viewed as the only way that like-minded people could obtain responsive government.

As the movement for township status developed, the families living in the area in and around Cornell's original lakefront subdivision cooperated in establishing the community's basic social institutions. Reflecting the Protestant leanings of the original inhabitants, a Presbyterian congregation was organized in 1858. At first its members met in a small chapel at the corner of Hyde Park and Oak (53rd), but in May 1860, they opened the First Presbyterian Church of Hyde Park on the same site. Eight years later the congregation erected another larger church at Adams (now Blackstone) and 53rd, turning the old building into a town hall, the basement of which became the village jail. Episcopalians, the only other religious denomination in Hyde Park in the early days, shared the quarters of the Presbyterians. A few years after Hyde Park Township was created, two other citizens joined Cornell in putting up the money to erect a small public grammar school at the intersection of 46th and Grand and, in 1870, Hyde Park villagers joined other township residents in paying for the construction of the first Hyde Park High School located at 50th and Lake (now Lake Park) Avenue.

Population growth remained modest through the 1860s with only 3,000 people estimated as residing in the township late in the decade. To speed growth and add to the amenities of the area, Cornell, shortly after the end of the Civil War, led a group of South Siders, many of whom also held land parcels which they wanted to develop, in pressing for the creation of a south parks system. In Springfield, Cornell lobbied for a bill that would create a South Park Commission empowered to sell bonds in an amount up to $1,000,000; to levy taxes on township residents to a maximum of $200,000 annually; and to use the money to purchase land and make improvements on a system of public parks and boulevards to serve South Siders. The bill was passed but was deemed defective by the voters, who objected to the looseness of

Hyde Park Water Works, 1884. Construction of the works began in 1882 at the southeast corner of 68th and Oglesby. This structure, the tunnel, and an intake crib nearly a mile into the lake, were completed two years later. The works did more than bring water to Hyde Park, they were a symbol of the township's independence from Chicago. From A. T. Andreas, *History of Cook County* (1884), CHS.

The Cottage Grove Avenue cable car line tied the Loop to Hyde Park. This 1903 photograph shows horses being used to move the cars after service was interrupted by a broken cable in the Douglas community. *Daily News* photo, gift of Field Enterprises, CHS.

several of its provisions. A referendum led to the defeat of the measure. Led by Cornell, the pro-park forces next joined the city's sanitary reformers and wealthy residents of the North and West sides who wanted park developments in their sections. Working separately and together these groups in 1869 petitioned the Illinois Assembly for the creation of three separate commissions to build the South Parks, West Parks, and Lincoln Park. For his contribution in getting the bills through the legislature, Cornell came to be recognized as "the father of the South Park system."

To plan the South Parks—which included Jackson and Washington parks, the Midway Plaisance, and adjacent boulevards—the South Park Commission hired America's best-known landscape architect, Federick Law Olmsted, who together with his partner Calvert Vaux was then working in Chicago laying out the suburban town of Riverside. Olmsted's grand design for the South Parks called for the transformation of raw prairie, marshes, and sand dunes into a recreational oasis, featuring equestrian drives, shaded walkways, and mirror lakes, all of which were to be enhanced by "aristocratic landscaping." The fire of 1871 set the project back, for it burned down the Tribune Building in which the offices of the South Park Commission were located and in which Olmsted's plans were stored. Nevertheless, Olmsted's basic ideas were retained, although in the 1870s the commission hired landscape architect H. W. S. Cleveland to trim some of the more expensive parts of the plan. Lack of money also held back development but by the mid-1880s the astute visitor to the city inevitably made a trip south out of the Loop along the boulevards and into Washington and Jackson parks to view the spectacular seasonal plantings.

What became the neighborhood of Hyde Park benefited in two ways from the development of the South Parks. First, the landscaped open spaces were within easy walking distance of every Hyde Park home and became a strong selling point for any real estate dealer attempting to sell a lot or house in the community. The parks also proved significant in another way, however. To the west, Washington Park served as a broad boundary separating Hyde Park from the corridor neighborhood which took its name from the park. As population moved south out of the stockyards and from the Near South Side, most of the inhabitants turned west moving into the neighborhoods of Grand Boulevard and Washington Park or farther south into Englewood. The Midway Plaisance, though narrower, provided the same kind of boundary on the south, while Jackson Park enhanced the effect of the lakefront to the east. Amid the changes and sometimes indistinct neighborhoods of the South Side, Hyde Park was blessed with three "natural boundaries" after 1869. These served to give Hyde Parkers a sense of physical definition for their community not found in many other South Side neighborhoods.

While the park and boulevard system was being installed, private companies were improving access to the township of Hyde Park and to Cornell's little community. In 1869 the Chicago and Calumet Railroad began operating a commuter line using "steam dummy" engines on 55th Street and Cottage Grove Avenue. This line connected with the South Side horsecar line at 39th Street. The Cottage Grove steam line gave the same kind of access to the western half of the little community as the Illinois Central gave to the eastern half. A year after the Chicago and Calumet line went into operation, the suburban town of Hyde Park had 1,000 inhabitants while the Hyde Park Township had 3,600.

Although these census figures demonstrate rapid growth, much of which had occurred during the last years of the decade, Cornell's Hyde Park continued to be dominated by businessmen and professionals. Some diversification in the population began to occur, however, when skilled artisans like carpenters and masons began to move into the neighborhood, attracted by the great amount of construction going on in the area. To serve the families living in the large houses owned by such substantial citizens as J. Young Scammon, lawyer-banker and founder of the Swedenborgian Church, music publisher Chauncy M. Cady, and Judge Van Hollis Higgins, a group of Irish and Scandinavian servants moved to Hyde Park, settling to the west of Saint Thomas the Apostle Roman Catholic Church located at 55th and Kimbark.

As the community grew, the leaders of Hyde Park Township saw a need for a more comprehensive form of government. Accordingly, in 1872, the township sent representatives to the General Assembly to state its needs. The legislature responded by granting the township a "village government," which allowed the township to expand services.

Most expensive for Hyde Parkers were problems connected with sewerage and the water supply, services imperative to protect public health at a time when cholera outbreaks were a constant threat. The township installed a water system in the early 1870s which proved inadequate before the end of the decade. The replacement system not only required a much larger intake pipe

5634–5640 S. Lake Park Avenue, 1950. These stores and apartment buildings were constructed in the early 1890s in anticipation of the World's Columbian Exposition held in Jackson Park in 1893. The alley near the right of the photograph was called Cable Court because it was a turnaround point for cablecars and later for the electric street railway. These buildings were eventually demolished as part of the Hyde Park Urban Renewal Project. Photo by Mildred Mead, CHS.

Southeast corner of 51st Street and University Avenue, 1951. Easy access to public transportation made this row of apartments, erected in the 1890s, attractive to commuters. The building originally had only two large apartments on each floor, but during the depression and the war that followed they were split up into numerous kitchenette units. Photo by Mildred Mead, CHS.

but had to be run farther out into the lake in order to avoid sweeping up the effluent that the township's sewers and drains were throwing into the water. The township also began to macadamize some of its streets, although on a minimal scale. By 1887 there were only 1.5 miles of surfaced street for each square mile of land in the township. Meanwhile, three fire stations, manned by volunteer companies, provided a measure of protection against flames for those who lived in Oakland, Kenwood, and Hyde Park, but other communities to the south were left to their own devices in case of serious fire. The police force also was minimal; only twenty-two officers and men protected the entire township in 1880. In that year the federal census found that the township's population had increased by more than 330 percent over the previous decade, reaching 15,800. During the next decade growth was even more phenomenal. The township's population rose by nearly 650 percent between 1880 and 1890 to 133,500. Hyde Park's most recent historian* summarized the results. By 1886, "the quiet little residential community pioneered by Paul Cornell and his friends had developed into a governmental monstrosity."

The massive growth of the 1880s demonstrated that the city had caught up with the township. Improved transportation played a part in the transformation. In 1887 the Cottage Grove Avenue cable car line was extended south to 67th, with a branch going eastward on 55th to Lake Park Avenue. Builders, anticipating the new and quicker form of transit, changed the character of the housing they constructed in the community. While Cornell's little village continued to attract some of Chicago's "best people" into the new large houses along Hyde Park Boulevard and Cornell Avenue,

fire maps indicate that row and town houses were also making their appearance in the community. Moreover, builders filled in some vacant lots along Hyde Park streets with workingmen's cottages. By 1890 the ideal which contemporary urban planners so fervently advocate—a diversity of housing stock catering to a variety of income levels—had become a reality in Paul Cornell's formerly elite suburb.

Housing was only one reason for the diversity, however. The Illinois Central stops in Hyde Park and the streetcar line along the western boundary and down 55th Street encouraged the development of the area as a commercial and professional service center. As the shopping centers at 53rd and Lake Park and 57th and Lake Park filled up, merchants scattered along Lake Park creating the beginning of a "strip commercial" street, easily accessible from either stop of the Illinois Central. Stores also moved west along 53rd, 55th, and 57th streets. Many of these buildings were two and three stories high with apartments on the upper floors. Hyde Park also obtained some industry during the 1880s. A large creamery with an attached ice house operated at the foot of 54th Street and, mixed in amid houses and apartment buildings, were small shops which manufactured wagon parts and carpets. A greenhouse could be found here and there and the car barns of the street railway line appeared as well.

Through the decade then, Hyde Park became an important commercial center on the South Side, a place where a person could see a doctor, get some lumber for home repairs, order coal, and shop for clothing, all in the course of an easy walk. Although Hyde Park had a population of 20,000 in the late 1880s there seem to have been more business establishments than its

own population warranted, indicating that people from Kenwood to the north, Washington Park to the west, and Woodlawn to the south came to Hyde Park to shop or purchase personal and professional services.

Having so many characteristics of a city population and facing numerous problems of an urban nature, the citizens of Hyde Park Township and of the area around Paul Cornell's original subdivision inevitably began to consider the advantages of becoming part of the city of Chicago. Yet when the issue was put to a vote in 1887 and again in 1889, the inhabitants of the village of Hyde Park and those of the township differed strongly about where their best interests lay. The township in each case favored annexation by the city of Chicago but the residents of the village of Hyde Park opposed it. The basis for the difference lay less in ideology than in the amount and quality of urban services enjoyed by those living in different parts of Hyde Park. Quite simply, the future neighborhood of Hyde Park, when compared to its counterparts in the township, was more than getting its money's worth. And both referenda, the first unsuccessful, the second successful in making Hyde Park Township part of the city, demonstrated that those who lived in the little town that Paul Cornell had started had no desire to become just one more neighborhood within Chicago.

Hyde Parkers had barely recovered from the annexation fights when two events accelerated the course of the community's development and added to the diversity of the area's population. In 1890 Chicago won the honor of hosting the celebration to honor Columbus's discovery of America

---

*   Jean F. Block, author of *Hyde Park Houses* (1978).

four hundred years earlier. Chicago architect Daniel H. Burnham, who headed the design group which was to build and landscape the exhibition, strongly urged that Jackson Park be the site for the fair. Frederick Law Olmsted, whose original scheme for the South Parks system had never been carried out, was consulted on how to accomplish the task of giving the fair a unified ground plan.

As construction of the grounds and fair buildings began, builders rushed to put up hotels and new stores around the fair grounds to serve the 300,000 visitors expected per day. Those trying to find sites for such buildings had to compete with other builders eager to build apartment- and flat-buildings around Jackson Park. In the process, Hyde Park acquired numerous hotels, apartment buildings, and cheaply built stores—most notably along Lake Park Avenue—in full view of those who would come to the fair on the Illinois Central.

Since all who visited the exposition would not be able to find accommodations in the immediate vicinity of the grounds, the transportation companies, urged on by a city eager for business, improved the means by which people who stayed in Loop hotels could get to the grounds in Hyde Park. The Illinois Central purchased more than forty new locomotives and 300 side-load commuter cars, while an elevated line was built from 12th Street south and then east on 63rd Street.

These new transportation connections, in concert with the building activity undertaken in anticipation of the fair, intensified trends already visible by 1890. Hyde Park was increasingly becoming a commercial and apartment neighborhood, following a course of development not unlike that of Grand Boulevard and Washington Park to the west.

Had this trend continued unchecked Hyde Park would have been caught in the same sweep of urban change as its neighbors. The difference stemmed from the fact that at this point the Baptist Church decided to establish a new University of Chicago along the north edge of the Midway Plaisance on land donated by Marshall Field—land which Field had been holding since 1879. Following its opening in 1892, the University of Chicago became the single most important factor in the history of the community. Committed from its inception to dealing with the city, blessed with a founder and faculty who viewed the university as having a broad urban mission, and anchored firmly to the Midway Plaisance and the South Parks system, the university began to dominate the development of Hyde Park.

Its first impact was on the housing market. Unlike Armour Institute, the university was not a commuter campus but an institution that encouraged its students, staff, and faculty to take up residence close by. Backed by John D. Rockefeller, William Rainey Harper, the university's first president, raided established faculty members from other institutions. Many of these new arrivals settled in Hyde Park. Within a decade the university's faculty and senior staff dominated Hyde Park south of 55th, while its students competed for housing throughout the neighborhood with newer immigrants who were moving south out of the stockyards and corridor community areas.

The university's research facilities and faculty attracted to Hyde Park a group of Chicago personalities ranging from poet Edgar Lee Masters and sculptor Lorado Taft to big-game hunter Mary Hastings Bradley and philanthropist Julius Rosenwald. Before the university came to Hyde Park the community was politically, socially, and economically conservative. Because of the kind of people it attracted, the neighborhood came to be dominated by people who were economically conservative, liberal on social issues, and politically independent. The stance was significant because it shaped the way that Hyde Parkers would later handle the urban problems which threatened to overwhelm the neighborhood.

During the period between 1890 and 1930, Hyde Park filled up, and in the process the neighborhood experienced its first taste of urban redevelopment as numerous small wooden houses were torn down to make way for new stores and for numerous apartment- and flat-buildings as well as some elegant residences. In the 1910s garages began to replace stables and the first significant number of automobiles appeared on the streets of Hyde Park. Newcomers abounded. The Irish still led among the foreign born in 1920 but Germans and recently arrived Russian Jews were also moving to the neighborhood in increasing numbers. Many of the latter two groups came by way of Grand Boulevard.

The 1920s were boom years for Hyde Park. Transportation access to the Loop was improved once more between 1923 and 1926 when the Illinois Central raised its grade all along the line and electrified it. At the same time, the railroad traded in the cars which it had bought to serve the World's Columbian Exposition patrons for new commuter coaches. By the mid-1920s the IC was running 165 trains to and from Hyde Park each day. A number of bus routes also were established during the decade, allowing easy access to the Loop from the western part of the neighborhood. Construction began on South Shore Drive, intended to provide a convenient lakefront route for motor traffic between the Loop and

Hyde Park. The area also benefited from a $15,000,000 expansion program carried out by the university. This led to the addition of both faculty and support positions. Finally, the community acquired new housing, principally in the form of apartment-hotels. More than two dozen high rises were constructed east of Dorchester Avenue, the largest group being east of the Illinois Central tracks. Two other high rises were built for other purposes. The Piccadilly Building contained a theater, street-level shops, and a hotel, while the Hyde Park Bank Building housed numerous professional offices as well as the financial institution from which it took its name.

The neighborhood's commercial facilities, however, failed to keep pace with these developments. The overall quality of shops deteriorated as neighborhood residents demonstrated their preference for using one of the numerous forms of transportation available to shop either in the Loop or in the expanding commercial center at 63rd and Halsted. The development of the Hyde Park artist's colony was a direct outcome of this decline. As aggressive retailers moved elsewhere to increase their sales, craftsmen, artists, and bookstores moved into the neighborhood's low rent storefronts, especially along Lake Park and on 57th Street east of Woodlawn. The presence of this group added a flavor of the Left Bank to Hyde Park.

The student population also needed cheap quarters and competed with as yet unrecognized artists for inexpensive rooms. Before long such established writers as Opie Read, Meyer Levin, Ben Hecht, and James T. Farrell also settled in the community, eventually drawing national attention to the place.

Through all of these developments the university's influence was pervasive. In 1925, a *Chicago Daily News* reporter pointed to the institution's role in ordering the process of change. "The university has exerted a powerful influence on the development of Hyde Park," the paper noted. "It has raised property values and tended to keep them stable. It has had the effect of zoning the community and preserving it against unfavorable encroachments."

The 1930 census showed the results of the boom: Hyde Park reported a total population of 48,017. The age distribution—20.1 percent under 19, 49.9 percent between 20 and 45, and 30 percent over 45—again demonstrated diversity. One group was especially prominent, however: German Jews who had been living on the avenues in earlier decades, especially along Grand Boulevard, had relocated in Hyde Park, particularly along Hyde Park Boulevard .(51st) and east of the Illinois Central Railroad tracks. Russian Jews had also entered the community. The Jewish presence in Hyde Park-Kenwood was reflected in the construction of the Kehilath Anshe Mayriv Temple at 900 East 50th Street in 1923.

The neighborhood was in delicate balance. The *Chicagoan* magazine, one of the Second City's numerous attempts to emulate the *New Yorker*, caught the situation and the unease that went with it. Hyde Park, the journal noted, was a place "where private residences have not wholly given way to apartment houses nor apartment houses to kitchenette apartment buildings, nor kitchenette apartments to cooperatives, but where everybody is wondering whether this is a cycle or a progression."

During the depression decade and the war that followed, Hyde Park's past caught up with it. Although a few new apartment buildings were constructed, that was not the main trend in housing. As some of the occupants of large family houses and apartments began to move out of the neighborhood, conversions of these spacious units into multiple smaller ones became more frequent and the population of the community rose, reaching 55,206 in 1950, an increase of nearly 15 percent. The age composition also changed, the number of those under 19 increasing by half and the number of those over 65 nearly doubling. Moreover, those who were arriving were poorer than the residents who had come in previous decades. Finally, while blacks constituted only 3 percent of Hyde Park's population in 1950, their presence represented the opening wedge of the South Side black belt which originated at the south edge of the Loop in the second decade of the twentieth century. Still, the most important change then, as later, was not in race but in economic levels. The poor had arrived in Hyde Park and with them came not only conflicts in life styles but a higher crime rate. What followed was the realization that if defensive steps were not taken, Hyde Park would be overwhelmed by the same fate that had overtaken the Near South Side, Douglas, and Oakland, and would become a slum.

Hyde Parkers were the first to recognize that radical surgery was necessary if the neighborhood was to be saved. Two organizations were formed to arrest the process of deterioration. The Hyde Park-Kenwood Community Conference was formed in 1949, initiated by the 57th Street Meeting of the Society of Friends. Its membership was broad, including Unitarians, Jews, and liberal citizens of various persuasions, who resided in both neighborhoods. The con-

5333–5345 S. University Avenue, 1951. These two single-family brick dwellings with wooden front porches were erected in Hyde Park during the 1910s. Apartment houses built in the same area during that decade and the next made these large homes architecturally anomalous. Photo by Mildred Mead, CHS.

5530–5534 S. Ellis Avenue, 1951. These three houses, all erected after 1890, represent the kind of in-fill housing built in Hyde Park near commercial centers and in areas where the demand for lots was weak. The subdivider narrowed the width of lots on this block to 24 feet—dimensions similar to those of lots in the working-class stockyards neighborhoods to the west. All three of these buildings were torn down in the course of urban renewal efforts. Photo by Mildred Mead, CHS.

ference proposed two objectives for Hyde Park: to stop decay and to advance racial integration. The South East Chicago Commission was organized in 1952. Backed by the University of Chicago it represented the more conservative residents of Hyde Park, including owners of businesses and professionals who had stores and offices in the neighborhood. The commission was oriented toward establishing the population of the neighborhood at a relatively high economic level. While their aims varied, the two groups avoided open clashes both because there was some overlapping membership and because they saw that unless they cooperated the situation in Hyde Park could only grow worse.

Backed by the university's resources and with many faculty and staff playing a part, the South East Chicago Commission evolved a plan of attack on the forces of decay. Nearly 43 acres bounded irregularly by 54th and 57th, Kimbark and Lake Park, were slated for wholesale demolition. Approximately two-thirds of the 1,419 dwelling units in that area were substandard, with 793 white families and 258 black families residing there. Another 4.6 acres of the 1,616 square acres of Hyde Park—the area along the north side of 54th from Blackstone to midway between Kenwood and Kimbark—also were slated for major demolition. Spot demolition and extensive rehabilitation were planned for housing that covered another 909 acres.

Demolition began in May 1955. The Chicago Land Clearance Authority spent $9,800,000 to acquire the buildings which were to be torn down to make way for private developers who would build new houses and a new shopping center for the community. The cooperation between city, university, and community residents to

make the project work was symbolized on May 10 when the wrecking ball struck the corner of the first building to be razed. Presiding at the occasion were Mayor Richard J. Daley and Lawrence A. Kimpton, chancellor of the University of Chicago and president of the South East Chicago Commission. Kimpton described the occasion as "historic," while Daley called it "one of the most important in the city's history."

For those who had to move because of the demolition and reconstruction that followed, that was little solace. Bruce Harlan, owner of a small department store, expressed the feelings of many of the shopowners who had to leave when the tearing down began when he said, "I'm pretty bitter, but I've quit yipping." An old resident for whom the relocation office of the Land Clearance Authority found adequate substitute quarters was more mellow. "I was sorry to see the old house go," he said, "but this is a job that has to be done." That was "the general feeling," according to *Chicago Sun-Times* reporter Ruth Moore.

As people moved away in anticipation of the wrecking ball, the population to the south moved in, taking up the temporary slack in the market. In 1950 only 3.1 percent of the population of Hyde Park was black. In the six-year period that followed, 20,000 whites left Hyde Park and neighboring Kenwood while 24,000 blacks moved in. For Hyde Parkers who were liberal on social issues it was not so much the color but the different economic and cultural background of the new arrivals that posed a problem. The newcomers were primarily poor persons brought up in the rural South, with little interest in maintaining the ambience that had grown up in Hyde Park during previous decades.

The federal censuses of 1950 and 1960

caught the neighborhood just before and during the urban renewal process. Over that decade the total number of housing units declined by only 307, but a 10 percent vacancy rate in anticipation of demolition resulted in a dramatic population drop of 17.4 percent from 55,206 to 45,577. Blacks made up 37.6 percent of the total population.

By the 1970s the impact of urban renewal was demonstrable in two ways. First, there were the new buildings, including the Hyde Park Shopping Center at the northwest corner of 55th Street and Lake Park Avenue, the numerous townhouses extending west on 55th and north and south of that street, and the two buildings of the University Apartments centered on a newly constructed mall on 55th Street. Meanwhile, Harper Court, a complex of small shops and restaurants, had been opened at the southwest corner of 52nd and Lake Park, while new high-rise apartments had been erected as far north on Lake Park as 47th Street.

The 1970 census provided a second kind of evidence of the changes that urban renewal had brought to the neighborhood. During the previous ten years, the number of dwelling units in Hyde Park had been reduced by 20.1 percent to 15,685, while the number of inhabitants had dropped even more sharply, by 37.6 percent, to 33,563. The racial composition of the population had also changed, from 37.6 percent black in 1960 to 31.0 percent in 1970. The median family income, meanwhile, had risen from $6,772 to $11,515, and the latter figure would have been even higher except for the large number of students included as part of the neighborhood's population. More revealing than the measure of median income, therefore, was the high percentage of families with incomes of over $10,000: 24.5 percent reported incomes between $10,00 and $15,000; 20.4 percent incomes between $15,000 and $25,000; and 10.0 percent earned between $25,000 and $50,000. Those of foreign stock remained a stable 27.0 percent of the population in 1960 and 26.9 percent in 1970. Among the foreign born, Germans and Asians predominated.

Hyde Park's urban renewal program thus appears to have accomplished its desired ends. Racial integration has been achieved and the trend toward the creation of a ghetto has been reversed. In the end, three factors worked to bring stability to the real estate market of the neighborhood. The first and most important was the University of Chicago. That institution owns over 150 parcels of land in Hyde Park, not counting the area on which instructional buildings stand. Of these, 17 are vacant lots, 12 are parking lots, and 2 are playgrounds. Five others are used for storage. Among the buildings owned by the university, 54 are single or multiple-unit faculty quarters, 26 are married student apartment buildings, 11 are used for single student housing, and 8 contain both student and non-student renters. Eight others are used for commercial purposes. As these figures suggest, the University of Chicago is the principal land and building owner in Hyde Park, and has used this leverage to keep the Hyde Park real estate market under control. The second factor is the presence of the black middle class. Hyde Park for decades has been a prestigious address for Chicago blacks who enjoyed the relatively tolerant atmosphere, accessible cultural activities, and excellent services of the neighborhood.

These factors alone would be sufficient to keep demand for housing there at a high level, but the fact that 70 percent of all the university's faculty also live in Hyde Park-Kenwood helps to keep demand for middle-

Frederick C. Robie House, 5757 S. Woodlawn Avenue, 1941. Frank Lloyd Wright designed this Prairie house for a Chicago motorcycle manufacturer who ordered a "fireproof, reasonably priced home to live in—not a conglomeration of doodads." Wright's design secured privacy for the family while allowing maximum exterior light penetration. Robie House was nearly torn down in 1957, but real estate developer William Zeckendorf purchased the structure and donated it to the University of Chicago. The building was designated a Chicago landmark in 1971. Photo by D. Wood Pease, CHS.

and upper-class housing high. In addition, another group has recently taken up what little slack there was in the Hyde Park market. Young married couples have purchased many of the smaller old houses in the neighborhood for major rehabilitation. The 1970 census demonstrated the effect of all these forces. The mean value of all owner-occupied units in 1970 was $40,332, and the mean contract rent was $144 per month. The citywide means in 1970 were $22,752 and $115, respectively.

The Hyde Park renewal effort is not without critics. These persons point out that the neighborhood lacks the diversity of former decades, that the range of stores has narrowed, and that the poor, especially blacks, were pushed out to make way for the redevelopment. Advocates of the program, meanwhile, retort that these measures have reduced crime, brought integrated living, and returned Hyde Park to the residential area that it was at the turn of the century. It takes both citizen interest and vast resources to make such an effort successful. The fact that Hyde Park was among the first American neighborhoods to engage in community renewal makes it all the more significant.

Chicago Tribune reporter Robert Cross provided an apt epilogue to the story of Hyde Park renewal in a 1975 article. "Nobody has ever claimed that Hyde Park would suit everyone," he wrote. "If somewhere along the line it lost some of its texture and sense of fun, at least it has turned out better than all those other rundown chunks of inner city that eventually became unfit habitats for anyone at all."

View northeast from 58th Street and Stony Island Avenue, 1951. The Museum of Science and Industry (originally the Palace of Fine Arts at the Columbian Exposition) is at the center of this photograph. Beyond are the Jackson Towers Apartments, the Promontory Apartments, and the Flamingo and Shoreland hotels. All of these high rises were erected in the 1920s, part of the apartment building boom around Jackson Park during that decade. Photo by Mildred Mead, CHS.

View northwest across part of the University of Chicago campus, Hyde Park, and Kenwood, 1960. Four structures dominate this photograph. At the lower left is the tower of Rockefeller Chapel, designed by New York architect Bertram Grosvenor Goodhue and finished in 1928 at a cost of $1,500,000, part of John D. Rockefeller's "final grant" to the University. In the lower center is the 165-foot Victor Fremont Lawson Tower, financed by Chicago publisher Victor Lawson, which is part of the Chicago Theological Seminary. Behind Lawson Tower is Mitchell Tower, presiding over the university complex which includes Hutchinson Commons, Reynolds Club, and Mandel Hall. At the center of the photograph is Stagg Field, named for football coach Amos Alonzo Stagg. Dedicated in 1913, Stagg Field later became the site for the Joseph Regenstein Library completed in 1970. Behind the stadium are parts of Hyde Park and Kenwood before urban renewal, as well as a section of Washington Park. Photo courtesy of Chicago Aerial Survey Company, CHS.

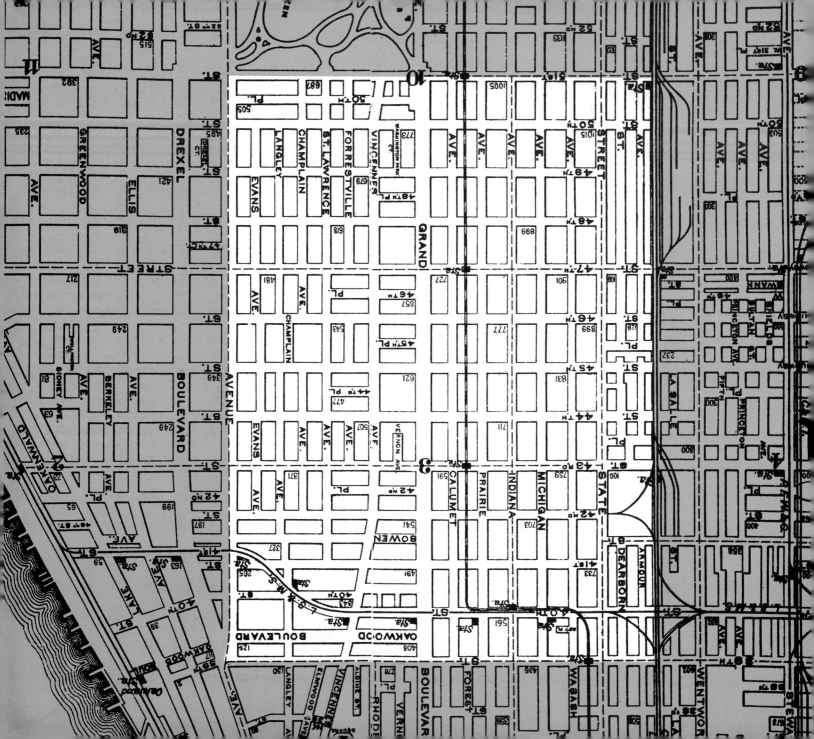

GRAND BLVD.

The community area of Grand Boulevard is bounded by Pershing Road (39th) on the north, 51st Street on the south, Cottage Grove Avenue on the east, and the tracks of the Chicago Rock Island and the Penn Central Railroad on the west. Unlike some of Chicago's community designations, this one has some basis in reality. This area, typically flat Illinois prairie, became part of Hyde Park when that town became a political unit in 1861. But during the decade after Hyde Park was created, many well-to-do Chicagoans moved south across the city's boundary to establish homes. The development of the South Parks system inspired growth in all directions and about 1870 a small scattered settlement appeared at the northwest corner of Washington Park. This hamlet became known as Forrestville, taking its name from the Forrestville School District which was formed in 1873. The bounds of that district were 43rd and 47th, between Cottage Grove Avenue and Indiana.

As part of their general plan, the South Park Commissioners widened Grand Boulevard (later South Parkway and eventually Dr. Martin Luther King, Jr. Drive) into a double-laned, landscaped carriage way. This improvement was carried out between 1874 and 1879 and real estate developers were quick to see its possibilities. The boulevard soon became a popular avenue for recreational carriage rides. Settlement along Grand Boulevard proceeded rapidly, with a few houses scattered east and west as well. By 1878 the Forrestville community had sufficient wealth to organize a volunteer fire company and buy a hose cart. Another innovation reflected the presence of German families—in December 1878 the small school district organized a kindergarten. A school census of 1882–83 reported the Forrestville population as 636. More than half of this number, 347, were 21 or over; 206 were between the ages of 6 and 21, and 83 were under 6. As these figures indicate, here was a "suburban frontier" town attracting young couples with children.

Excellent transportation connections with the city encouraged further settlement in Forrestville. Cable cars ran south on Cottage Grove Avenue to 39th Street by 1882, and within five years the line had reached 63rd Street. East and west cross lines connected the area with the well-to-do sections on the lakeshore and with the growing industries in the stockyards area along the South Branch of the Chicago River. In 1896 the State Street and Indiana Avenue car lines were electrified, and the South Side elevated began making stops in the neighborhood at 43rd, 47th, and 51st streets.

The annexation of 1889 made this area part of the city of Chicago. Under the name of Grand Boulevard it soon developed into a middle-class neighborhood of single-family dwellings and three-story apartment houses.

The first settlers had been native-born Americans descended from immigrants who had come from Scotland, Ireland, and England. Within a few decades these residents were joined by others from the same groups who made their way south "down the boulevards" from the central city. As early as 1881 Catholics established a parish on the corner of 41st and Wabash. St. Elizabeth of Hungary was founded by the Reverend D. J. Riordan who had come to Chicago from Ireland in 1848. The first meeting place for this congregation was a small frame building that had once served as the spiritual home for St. Anne's parish before a new church was erected. By 1892 St. Elizabeth's parish served 1,000 families. Nine years later the Paulist Fathers started a mission for non-Catholics there, as a result of which St. Elizabeth's gained a reputation for making large numbers of converts to Catholicism. This activity continued into the early 1920s when the number of congregants was declining and the parish neighborhood was experiencing the first stages of racial change.

Catholics founded a second parish in Grand Boulevard in 1901. To begin with, the newly formed congregation met in a rented building at 49th and Grand Boulevard. Corpus Christi communicants celebrated their first mass on Christmas Day, 1915, in a new building at 49th and Grand Boulevard. Membership in the parish was already declining even as the new edifice was opened for worship.

Around the turn of the century Jewish residents began to make their home in the Grand Boulevard neighborhood. Many were members of Sinai Temple, Chicago's first reform synagogue, founded in 1861. Two years later it had moved to Plymouth Court and Van Buren, and, shortly thereafter, to Wabash and Peck Court. After the latter building was destroyed by the fire of 1871, the Sinai congregation made its first move to the South Side, holding services at Martin's Hall at 22nd and Indiana until 1876, when a new synagogue was completed at 21st and Indiana. This building was enlarged in 1892. By the turn of the century many members of this congregation had already moved farther south into the Grand Boulevard neighborhood. Other Jewish institutions were also moving south: the Standard Club from 16th and Michigan to 24th and Michigan, and the Lake Side Club from 31st and Indiana to 42nd and Grand Boulevard. Sinai Temple itself moved to 46th and Grand in 1915. Within a decade, however, many members of the congrega-

tion had moved farther south and eventually the temple was put up for sale. Not until 1944 was a buyer found. A new Sinai Temple was dedicated in 1950 at 54th and South Shore Drive in Hyde Park.

Blacks began to move into Grand Boulevard in the 1890s, residing first near 46th and Langley and 46th and Champlain. In 1895 the great majority of blacks lived north of 31st Street, on State, Dearborn, and Federal, and important black institutions like Bethel Church, Quinn Chapel, and Olivet Baptist Church were organized in this area of the city. As the number of blacks in Chicago increased rapidly during World War I, the black belt was pushed southward. These population changes in turn produced institutional changes like those that occurred in other South Side neighborhoods. In 1920, for example, a black congregation purchased the Ebenezer Baptist Church, located at 45th and Vincennes Avenue, from its white congregants, who had moved away.

The Catholic Church responded to the increase in the number of blacks in the city by forming a black congregation, the parish of St. Monica, in 1885. This group of communicants originally met in the basement of St. Mary's in the Loop. By 1889 St. Monica's had sufficient funds to undertake a building campaign and four years later the parish opened a chapel at 36th and Dearborn. For many years, St. Monica's, which soon organized a school as well, was the only black Catholic parish in the city. Within a decade of its founding, however, blacks were also attending the parishes of St. Elizabeth and Corpus Christi. The latter church also played an important role in black Catholic education, founding the Chicago Industrial School for Girls in 1889 at 49th and Indiana. In August 1911 the

students of that school were transferred to new quarters in Des Plaines, Illinois. The Sisters of the Good Shepherd then went on to found the Illinois Technical School for Colored Girls at the original site. Corpus Christi was the home parish for this institution, which, in 1916, had an enrollment of 115 students.

Corpus Christi fell on hard times after the neighborhood experienced racial change and the Franciscans reorganized it as a predominantly black parish in 1932. In the early 1960s the Franciscan Order purchased the former site of the College of St. Xavier at 49th and Cottage Grove Avenue, and established Hales Franciscan High School. This boys' school continues to serve the black community on the South Side.

Between 1918 and 1920 blacks moved into Grand Boulevard in a surge that brought a number of incidents of racial violence. By 1920, 32 percent of the area's 87,005 inhabitants were black. Among the foreign born, Irish and German Jews still predominated. A decade later, 94.6 percent of all the 103,256 residents in Grand Boulevard were black. Italians, Germans, Russian Jews, and Irish predominated among the whites remaining in the neighborhood. Population increase was slower in the 1940s, the total number of inhabitants in Grand Boulevard reaching 114,557 by 1950. But in the course of that decade the racial transformation of the area was completed and the census of 1950 showed a population that was 99 percent black. During the 1950s demolition of dilapidated housing by the Chicago Land Clearance Authority reduced the population by 30 percent. In 1960 Grand Boulevard still had 80,036 inhabitants and the 1970 total of only 98 more indicated that the neighborhood had reached a population plateau.

Elevated station at 43rd Street, looking west from Calumet Avenue, 1925. Workers employed in the Michigan Southern Railroad yards close by had erected houses along this section of 43rd even before the construction of the South Side elevated in 1892. The "L" intensified commercial development on this street. Photo gift of the Chicago Transit Authority, CHS.

Northwest corner of 48th and State streets, 1956. These stone-fronted brick commercial and apartment buildings were erected during the 1880s. The Rock Island Railroad and the State Street cable car line provided easy transportation but an unattractive residential environment. These buildings were eventually torn down to make way for the Robert Taylor Homes. Photo by Shirley J. Stone, CHS.

In the late 1970s it is difficult to recognize that Grand Boulevard once was the cultural and business center of black Chicago. Between 1900 and 1915 the area around 31st and State was the main business district for blacks. By the latter year, this commercial center had shifted to 35th Street in Douglas. A decade later, it extended along 47th between St. Lawrence and Indiana Avenue, centering on Grand Boulevard.

Of special significance was the Regal Theater at the intersection of 47th and Grand Boulevard, which for more than two decades featured some of the foremost black entertainers in the country, including Nat King Cole, Duke Ellington, Louis Armstrong, Cab Calloway, Ethel Waters, and Lena Horne. In 1973 the Chicago Land Clearance Authority demolished this landmark along with many other commercial structures. The loss of the Regal Theater was deeply felt by black Chicagoans. As one story in the *Chicago Tribune* of September 6, 1973, noted, "Growing up black on the South Side is synonymous with knowing and loving the Regal."

The demolition of the Regal had an economic consequence as well. In combination with the earlier loss of higher income patrons, its destruction dealt a heavy blow to the 47th Street business district. The two principal shopping centers for South Side blacks now are at 63rd and Halsted and in the Loop.

Because Grand Boulevard was such an important black neighborhood, an early private philanthropic housing effort there was the more significant. In 1929, Julius Rosenwald, former head of Sears, Roebuck and Company, provided $2,700,000 for the construction of a 16-story building containing 453 apartments on the block bounded by Michigan, 47th, Wabash, and 46th. Rosenwald believed that it should be possible to provide reasonably priced housing for blacks with relatively low incomes and at the same time get a fair return on his investment. The Great Depression engulfed the country as the project opened and in the first six years Rosenwald's return was only 1.15 percent per year. In 1957 the project was sold to a non-profit corporation, Michigan Boulevard Apartments, Inc., and put under professional management.

Between 1960 and 1964, 3,199 housing units were added to Grand Boulevard's housing stock, most of which were built with public money. The largest of these undertakings, the Robert Taylor Homes, is located west of State Street between 39th Street and 54th Place. The architectural firm of Shaw, Metz and Associates designed 28 buildings, each being 16 stories high, which together contain more than 4,300 units. This project was especially significant, because it contained more 3- and 4-bedroom units than other public housing projects built during the same period. Consequently, eligible families with a large number of children were likely to be assigned to these rather than to other buildings by the Chicago Housing Authority. In 1971, 77 percent of the 27,000 persons who lived in the Robert Taylor Homes were under the age of 18. Public housing units

Michigan Boulevard Garden Apartments, 54 E. 47th Street, 1951. Philanthropist Julius Rosenwald hired Ernest Grunsfeld, Jr. (the architect who created Adler Planetarium) to design this project for upwardly mobile blacks. Grunsfield planned more than 400 apartments in five-story walk-up buildings arranged around a central courtyard. More than $2.7 million was spent on the project, which opened in 1929. Photo by Mildred Mead, CHS.

now make up over 15 percent of all the homes in the Grand Boulevard community area. The remainder of the housing stock is old, most of it having been constructed before 1920.

The population of Grand Boulevard is growing both younger and older at the same time. In 1950 those 18 and under constituted 24.1 percent of the total. Two decades later that number had risen to 42.6 percent. Meanwhile, during the same two decades, those aged 65 and over had increased from 5.6 percent to just over 11 percent of the neighborhood population. The area is also characterized by low income: 35.4 percent of all inhabitants reside in households with family income under $5,000, and 36.5 percent in households with incomes between $5,000 and $10,000.

The way in which Grand Boulevard residents acquire their income demonstrates that underemployment rather than public aid is the chief factor in the area's low income levels. In 1970, fewer than 1 percent of Grand Boulevard families were on public aid, compared with 4.8 percent for the city as a whole. Another 16.1 percent of the families obtained their income from social security or railroad retirement, while 21.8 percent were self-employed. This latter figure compares with the citywide figure of 4.5 percent. Employment in local government also is important, with 5.7 percent of the males and 10 percent of the females working for local government agencies. In sum, the neighborhood is basically a black lower working-class community with a very young population.

Along with these attributes, two other sets of statistics stand out as particularly significant. Nearly 93 percent of all housing units in Grand Boulevard are apartments. Given the age structure of the population, it should be anticipated that people who live in this neighborhood frequently change places of residence. The 1960 census showed that 57.1 percent of all community area families had moved in the previous five years. The comparable figure for 1970 was 51.4 percent. Grand Boulevard, then, functions as a high mobility corridor or access neighborhood through which blacks pass as rapidly as did the whites who preceded them.

Such neighborhoods suffer from a high degree of instability. Massive demolition and new construction of public housing have succeeded in updating the housing stock of the area but have done little to stabilize the population living there. The fact that the percentage of those aged 65 and over is rising rapidly would seem to suggest that there will be less movement than previously, but the overwhelming presence of the Robert Taylor Homes, with its many units capable of holding large families, works in the opposite direction. It is unlikely that this basic pattern of movement will change very much in the next few decades without major public intervention.

St. Xavier College, 4900 S. Cottage Grove Avenue, 1953. The Sisters of Mercy opened the first St. Xavier's Academy for Girls in the Loop in 1846 and by the time of the fire they were educating girls from nursery school through college. After 1871 St. Xavier's moved to a new location at 29th Street and Wabash Avenue, then in 1901 to the building shown here. In 1955 the institution moved again, this time to a 155-acre tract bounded by 99th and 103rd streets, Central Park Avenue, and Pulaski Road. Photo by J. Sherwin Murphy, CHS.

Provident Hospital, 426 E. 51st Street, 1960.
Founded by black physician Daniel Hale
Williams in 1891 in a two-story house at 29th
and Dearborn, Provident Hospital moved to
a larger house seven years later. Not until 1933
was the present 200-bed facility built.
Provident was the first hospital in Chicago with
black physicians on its staff. When formerly
all-white hospitals began to accept black
patients Provident became more or less a
charity facility. Now, after many years of
fundraising, rehabilitation of this hospital has
finally begun. Photo by Herb Kahn, CHS.

Ludwig van Beethoven Elementary School,
25 W. 47th Street, 1962. This 42-
room school was opened in 1962, serving
mainly the residents of the nearby Robert Taylor
Homes. Photo by Herbert Wallace, CHS.

View northwest from 43rd Street at Wabash Avenue, 1952. This Sunday morning photograph captures the activity at St. Paul's Church of God and Christ (the low brick building near the upper right). Just north of the church is the old Henry B. Clarke house, the rectory and community house for the congregation. The Clarke house had been built in 1836 at 16th and Prairie and was moved to this location in 1871; it has recently been moved back to the Prairie Avenue Historic District. The parked automobiles which line Wabash Avenue are one indication of the heavy residential density of the area. Photo by Mildred Mead, CHS.

The Regal Theater, view south on Grand Boulevard after World War II. The elegant sweep of Grand Boulevard provided an appropriate setting for the Byzantine façade of this theater, erected in 1927 by Balaban and Katz specifically for the South Side black population. As one nostalgic Chicagoan recalled when the Regal was scheduled for demolition in 1973, "If a guy took you to a stage show at the Regal and dinner at the Rumpus Room—and he could do it then for about $5—you were something special. . . ." Photo courtesy of the Theatre Historical Society.

WASHINGTON

PARK

THE SOUTH OPEN GREEN

GREEN HOUSE

PAVILION

THE DEER PADDOCK

WASHINGTON
PARK CLUB

MIDWAY

UNIVERSITY OF CHI

GYMNASIUM

BOULEVARD

9   10   11

16   15   14

WASHINGTON PARK

The community area of Washington Park is named for the recreational area which forms its eastern boundary. The western border is the combined tracks of the Penn Central and Rock Island lines. The neighborhood's southern edge is an irregular line running from Cottage Grove Avenue west on 60th to South Park Avenue, then on South Park to 63rd, 63rd to State, from State to 61st, and along 61st to where it intersects the railroad lines. These irregularities were necessary to fit the community in around the Penn Central yards in Englewood. The northern boundary, 51st Street, is very arbitrary, for Garfield Boulevard (55th Street), which cuts east and west through the community, offers at least as significant a breaking point as does 51st.

The first settlement in Washington Park resulted from the presence of the Rock Island Railroad yards which were located northwest of the community between 47th and 51st in 1856. Over the next fifteen years a number of Irish and some Germans who were employed in these yards established a small settlement north of 55th and west of State. This group of settlers built their houses sufficiently far apart to engage in truck farming while holding jobs in the Rock Island yards. The predominance of the Irish in Washington Park may be inferred from the fact that the first religious organization in the area was St. Anne's parish established by the Catholic church in 1865.

The next development that brought people to Washington Park was the building of the South Parks system after 1869. Although Paul Cornell's Hyde Park and Dr. John A. Kennicott's Kenwood were the principal beneficiaries of the laying out of Jackson Park, the Midway Plaisance, and Washington Park, the community area named after the latter park also received new settlers. Developers were quick to see the advantages of laying out broad avenues extending northward from Washington Park toward the built-up city of Chicago. Grand Boulevard, Calumet, Indiana, and South Michigan were all influenced by the presence of Washington Park and its adjacent recreational grounds. The result was that while workers who labored in the nearby railroad yards dominated the western portion of the neighborhood, the wealthy came to live along the avenues in the eastern half of the community.

Scattered construction in the area that became the Washington Park community continued through the 1870s and early 1880s. Then another focal point of activity was developed at the southeast corner of the future neighborhood. Almost from the time that the South Parks system had been established, well-to-do South Siders pressured the Park Commission for construction of a racecourse on which they could run their own thoroughbreds as well as have a place for professional racing. In 1884 a group of wealthy Chicagoans chartered a private sporting club dedicated to breeding and racing thoroughbreds. With Civil War hero General Philip Sheridan fronting for them, the small group of promoters had no difficulty in raising the money to construct the track, stables, and clubhouse of the Washington Park Race Track. Located between 61st and 63rd and Cottage Grove Avenue and South Park in what is now the community of Woodlawn, the Washington Park track was the most prestigious in the city for nearly two decades. Its annual season opener, the American Derby for three-year-olds, offered the largest single racing purse in the nation. For Chicago's high society, the Derby was the major outdoor social event of the year, drawing huge crowds to watch the races and view the city's elite at play. After a betting scandal and a murder at another race track in 1894, the Washington Park racecourse was closed for three seasons. It reopened in 1898 and continued in operation until 1905 when a city-wide drive against gambling forced the closing of all racetracks inside the city limits.

While it operated, however, the seasonal activity at the track stimulated the formation of a business district which included a number of saloons and betting parlors plus a small community of inhabitants along 63rd Street in the southeast corner of the neighborhood. During this period, numerous elegant mansions were constructed along South Parkway, the major boulevard maintained by the South Park Commissioners.

Two years before the Washington Park community was annexed to Chicago as part of Hyde Park, the Cottage Grove Avenue cable car line was extended south to 67th Street, and the State Street line reached 63rd. The former line ran along the eastern boundary of the neighborhood, the latter cut through its western third. The community area's transportation access was improved in 1892 when the South Side elevated reached 55th. The following year it would be extended to Jackson Park, the site of the Columbian Exposition. In 1907 the Englewood "L" was tied into the Jackson Park line, completing the South Side rapid transit system.

These transportation connections encouraged extensive residential and commercial development in Washington Park. Between 1890 and 1893 preparations for the Columbian Exposition helped fill the avenues west of South Park with buildings, and by the time of the fair the corridor of north-south streets between State and Indiana as far south as 55th was lined with fine homes and elegant apartment houses. Even with this construc-

tion, however, a considerable amount of land in the community remained undeveloped. An oak woods between 56th and 59th, Indiana and Calumet, for example, served as a meeting and social gathering place for farmers from the surrounding area. Only a few families lived south of 55th and east of State, notably along 59th, and on Indiana and Wabash. This latter area was not developed until the decade after 1895 when apartment buildings were constructed there. That also was the fate of the area north of 55th and east of Indiana. This section became an enclave of buildings appropriately named "honeymoon flats," because they were the first homes for numerous newlyweds. Even with the construction of these apartment houses, however, single-family homes predominated in Washington Park until the turn of the century. After that the apartments took over. By 1915 the community had reached residential maturity.

A number of commercial areas served the residents of Washington Park. Several of these were to be found around stops of the elevated which cut through the neighborhood between Calumet and State. Small groups of convenience stores, for instance, sprang up around the terminals at 51st, 55th, 58th, and 61st, while another shopping center could be found to the west at 59th and State, on the Englewood line. Two other stops were located at the southern edge of the neighborhood at 63rd and South Park, and at 63rd and Cottage Grove. Thus the pattern in Washington Park was one of a number of retail centers rather than a single dominant shopping core or street. If residents wanted a wider choice of merchandise, they went either to 47th Street or to 63rd, especially to the 63rd and Halsted shopping center.

This multinodal shopping pattern reflect-

ed the lack of a dominant identity which had been characteristic of the Washington Park area from its beginning. The singular feature that was shared by most of the neighborhood residents was their willingness to settle elsewhere as soon as they had children and the money to make the move. Yet the wealthy population which lived in the mansions and elegant apartments along the avenues was relatively stable, while to the west the railroad yards continued to provide steady employment.

The Washington Park area's relative instability was exacerbated by the activities of the entertainment district which developed along its southern edge. As the Washington Park Race Track was in its last phase of operation, the Sans Souci (French for "free from care") Amusement Park opened in the block of Cottage Grove, 60th, Langley, and 61st Street. From the beginning, Sans Souci's principal attraction "was its beer garden facing a band shell." As one writer described it, "Here South Siders could sit around small tables under trees, sip their beer . . . and listen to Creatore's Band giving their all to the 1812 Overture."

During the last year of racing at the Washington Park track, the White City Amusement Park, which took its name from the popular appellation for the Columbian Exposition of 1893, opened its gates in Washington Park, offering entertainment for the masses. In the course of its sixteen-year history more than 35 million visitors thronged through its turnstiles.

After being partially burned in 1910, Sans Souci Park fell on hard times. In 1914 Frank Lloyd Wright was commissioned to design an entertainment complex including a ballroom, restaurant, and outdoor theater on the northeast corner of the Sans Souci Park

Washington Park, 1889. Landscape gardeners employed by the various parks competed with each other to create impressive floral displays of the kind shown here. CHS.

Clubhouse at Washington Park Race Track, 1891. "I remember," an old-timer recalled in 1951, "how we used to gather on Grand Boulevard on American Derby day and watch the wonderful array of tallyhos and tandems on their way to the track." Once there, the young blades who drove these elegant equipages paraded them in front of admiring friends gathered in and around the luxurious clubhouse. CHS.

block. Named Midway Gardens, this elegant place offered fine food, symphonic music, and ballet performances by such stars as Pavlova. Unfortunately, Midway Gardens had only one successful season before the war in Europe dampened Chicago's night-life. Unable to recover even their original investment, the owners of Midway Gardens sold it to the Edelweiss Brewing Company in 1916. The Chicago beer concern was less interested in high-class entertainment than it was in selling food and drink, and trans-formed Midway into "an overgrown beer garden, catering to a lower class of pa-trons." In spite of the shift in emphasis, attendance at Midway Gardens had already declined even before prohibition became law in January, 1920. The Midway Gardens changed ownership once more and was transformed into a garage and car wash. It was finally torn down in 1929.

The White City Amusement Park, mean-while, enjoyed steady popularity through the first half of the 1920s, primarily by capi-talizing on the dance craze then sweeping the nation. A competitor for the dance business, the Trianon Ballroom, opened its doors at 62nd and Cottage Grove Avenue in 1922. The White City Amusement Park was partially burned in 1927 and never really recovered from the fire. In 1933 it went into receivership, and six years later was condemned. At the Trianon, mean-while, the fun continued for another twelve years or so as thousands of Chicagoans danced the night away or met their future mates. This elegant ballroom finally closed in 1952.

These entertainment facilities attracted thousands of strangers through Washington Park, at first by horse, then mechanical transit, and eventually by auto. By the be-ginning of World War I, these visitors were passing through an area filled with apart-ment houses rather than a neighborhood of single-family dwellings. At the time of the 1930 census only 4.9 percent of all housing units in the Washington Park area were occupied by their owners. Because the per-centage of apartments was so high individ-ual families tended to move in and out of the neighborhood faster than home owners would have done. This tendency increased as the apartments became older and as units were subdivided and rents became cheaper. The result was that ethnic and racial transitions in Washington Park took place with extraordinary rapidity.

White Protestants moved into Washington Park in large numbers in the years after the Columbian Exposition, dominating the area east of State. Their quick passage through the area can be traced in the movement of one Methodist congregation, the State Street Methodist Church, which in 1900 sold its building at 47th and State in the Grand Boulevard area to a black congrega-tion which renamed the church St. Mark Methodist. The State Street Methodist con-gregation, meanwhile, moved to 50th and Wabash, about four blocks south of its earlier location and changed the name of its church to St. Andrew's Methodist. In 1910 the congregation moved once more, this time to a new building at the corner of 57th and Indiana in Washington Park. At that time the congregants adopted the new name of Woolley Memorial Methodist Church in honor of Mrs. Katherine Woolley, who gave $10,000 toward completion of the new building.

Jews had begun to filter into the neigh-borhood of Washington Park as early as the 1890s, settling near the elevated stops. This specific movement was part of a more gen-eral exodus of affluent German Jews from the center of the city. The movement of Jews through the Washington Park area can be seen in a brief history of the Ohavo Amuno congregation. In 1872 this group was located in a building at Clark and Polk streets near what is now Dearborn Station. In 1918 this congregation moved to 4819 South Michigan, purchasing a building from the First South Park Presbyterian Church. Nine years later the Ohavo Amuno congregation merged with the Conservative South Side Hebrew Temple. The latter group had been organized in 1888 and occupied a building at 59th and Michigan. The reason for the merger was declining membership in both congregations. By 1925 the South Side congregation had lost about fifty members who had moved to South Shore and rented a hall on 71st and Clyde where they held services until they could erect a synagogue on a lot which they had purchased at 74th and Chappell. Jews who were interviewed in 1927 about the continued black movement into the Washington Park area stated that they in-tended to hold services at the 59th and Michigan Avenue synagogue so long as they could muster the requisite ten adult male members. But parents who had al-ready moved farther south were refusing to send their children back to the temple for religious instruction because Washington Park was a black neighborhood.

The initial black settlement of Washing-ton Park occurred in the 1880s when the area was open farmland. During that de-cade a few black families built houses on Lafayette Street south of 55th, about mid-way between the Rock Island yards, which ran northward from 47th, and the Pennsyl-vania yards, which ran in a southeasterly direction from 61st. During the great expan-sion of Chicago's black population which began in 1915, some blacks entered Washington Park by moving south and east from the end of the "black belt" at 39th between the Rock Island yards and State Street. Meanwhile, the black enclave south of 55th Street expanded, running south to 59th, but was limited by State Street on the east. Wentworth, the first street west of the tracks, remained essentially white until well after the depression decade. After the 1919 race riot, there was a small easterly movement on Garfield Boulevard to its intersection with Michigan Avenue. By 1920 Washington Park had 38,076 residents, of whom 15 percent were black. Ten years later, the population was 44,016, with 92 percent black. White Protestants who had lived on the avenues, Irish Catholics who lived west of State, and the Jews who had started out in the shadows of the elevated, had moved on. The wartime decade merely prolonged the period of racial change. In 1950 the community's population had grown by 29 percent to reach 58,856, with blacks making up 99 percent of the total.

As Washington Park became an all-black ghetto, the distinctions between income groups that had characterized the area when it was all white continued as before. State Street, which had been the division between working class and middle class, remained a break line, with blacks east of that street regarding those to the west of the street as inferior. This negative connotation attached especially to the original pioneers on Lafayette south of 55th and certainly to those who lived in the ramshackle wooden and brick shanties that lined Federal Street just east of the Rock Island Railroad tracks. When poor Irish and German railroad workers resided there in earlier decades, the Federal Street slum was already one of the most notorious in the city. The arrival of blacks changed its color, not its character.

During the 1950s and 1960s the Chicago Land Clearance Authority began demolition in Washington Park. The section west of State, including the Federal Street slum, was leveled and replaced with public housing. Spot demolition occurred in other parts of the community area as well. The results showed in the housing figures. Between 1950 and 1970 the number of housing units in Washington Park dropped from 16,477 to 15,890, a decline of 3.6 percent. Of that 1970 total, 16.3 percent of the units had been built after 1950. Included among these was that portion of the Robert Taylor Homes located between State and the Rock Island tracks, 51st and 54th Place. These were completed in 1962. The year before, some publicly financed apartments for the elderly had opened on various scattered sites in the neighborhood.

The net effect of these changes in the housing stock was first to decrease and then to increase the area population. Starting from a high of 56,856 in 1950, the neighborhood's total number of inhabitants dropped by 23 percent to 43,690 a decade later. With some improvement in housing stock through public housing, including the construction of some units for larger families, Washington Park's population rose by 5.2 percent to reach 46,024 in 1970 with 99 percent of the total black.

By 1970 Washington Park was still a highly mobile neighborhood. More than 53 percent of those then living there had moved to the unit they were then occupying since 1965, the same percentage as had moved between 1955 and 1960. Moreover, 35.0 percent of all Washington Parkers were Southern born, indicating that the neighborhood is a receiving area for many such blacks when they first arrive in Chicago. Also, many of the area's families had low incomes: while 17.5 percent of all families earned between $10,000 and $15,000, 28.3 percent earned under $5,000. Moreover, the number of children in Washington Park was high, with 38.0 percent being 18 or under. In neighboring Gage Park and Hyde Park this age group accounts for only 25.3 and 19.1 percent of the total populaton, respectively. Rents in the Washington Park area were relatively high, with the mean rental being $101 per month. This is considerably higher than the comparable figures in white working-class neighborhoods: $80 in McKinley Park, $75 in Bridgeport, and $66 in New City.

The Washington Park area continues to face an uncertain future. Much of the housing is old and in need of repair and, in some cases, total renewal. The park from which the community took its name and excellent transportation connections with the central business district remain the two basic attractions of the community. It is also close to the University of Chicago in Hyde Park, but whether or not the renewal that is spreading along the South Side lakefront will move westward to include Washington Park remains in question. In the end, its variant beginnings, the lack of a single community identity, and the preponderance of apartments over single-family units have been decisive factors in shaping the evolution of Washington Park. These factors will have to be dealt with by deliberate policy if positive change is to be brought to the area.

Vermont Hotel, 810–18 Hyde Park Boulevard, 1893. This was one of many hotels and rooming houses erected in preparation for the World's Columbian Exposition; it was later converted to apartments. The Drexel Monument can be seen to the right. From *The Graphic*, 1893, CHS.

Old Vienna Restaurant and Buffet, southwest corner of Cottage Grove Avenue and 60th Street, ca. 1900. Near the turn of the century small commercial establishments like this one appeared strung along both sides of Cottage Grove from its intersection with 63rd Street. CHS.

Southwest corner of 58th Street and Indiana Avenue, ca. 1906. These two three-story buildings were erected before World War I, one block east of the Carter Public School and one-half block north of St. Edmund's Episcopal Church. Garages were added at the back in the 1920s. Photo by Charles E. Barker, CHS.

Union Central Baptist Church, 5520 S. State Street, 1952. This storefront church was one of many black social and cultural institutions that appeared along State Street from the 1920s onward. Photo by Arthur M. Weiland, CHS.

Entrance to White City Amusement Park, 63rd Street and South Park Avenue, ca. 1925. This entertainment center opened on May 19, 1906, in what was then a semi-rural area. Nightly fireworks, rides, spectaculars, dancing, and a variety of other amusements brought 35 million people here during the first sixteen years of the park's operation. CHS.

ARMOUR SQUARE

Located to the west of Douglas and the Near South Side and east of Bridgeport, the community area of Armour Square is twenty-one blocks long and only four or five blocks wide. While technically it is bounded along its northern edge by the South Branch of the Chicago River and 18th Street, in fact it is cut off along that edge by railroad yards which connect with Dearborn Station to the north. Steel rails also mark its eastern and western boundaries. The combined tracks of the Chicago and Western Indiana and the Penn Central are on its western side while those of the Chicago, Rock Island, and Pacific run along its eastern edge. Pershing Road is its southern border. The northern half of Armour Square was annexed to the City of Chicago in 1853, while the southern half was absorbed ten years later. The community derives its name from a little park that lies between 33rd and 34th, with Wentworth on the east and Shields on the west. This park was opened in 1904.

Urban settlement began in Armour Square during the 1860s. The portion of the corridor neighborhood north of 35th Street was settled during the Civil War. From the beginning the population of this neighborhood was linked with that of Bridgeport and was mainly composed of working-class Irish and Germans, with a few Swedes arriving soon after the other two groups. The southern half of the neighborhood began to be built up after the opening of the Union Stock Yard in 1865. Throughout the 1860s, the typical dwelling unit constructed was the wooden balloon-frame house. This mode of building received new emphasis when the city established fire limits after the 1871 holocaust. The exclusion of wooden structures from the inner city meant that poorer persons who could not afford brick houses were shoved to the edge of the built-up area into neighborhoods like Armour Square where cheap wooden-frame structures could still be erected.

The first group strong enough to form neighborhood institutions were the German Lutherans. In early 1862 one such group held its first service in a school building at 20th and Wentworth. Within six months, this congregation erected a church on a leased lot at 21st and Archer. This building was dedicated in November 1862 as the Third German United Evangelical Salem Lutheran Church. A few years later this congregation purchased a lot at the corner of 24th and Wentworth and moved the Salem Church building to this location. Shortly thereafter, however, the congregation split over ideological issues. The dissident group broke away to form the Evangelical Lutheran St. Stephen's Church at 25th and Wentworth. St. Stephen's held its first services in February 1871.

Another group of Germans organized the Methodist Tyng Mission in 1869, meeting in a building at Archer and Wentworth. To aid the Tyng congregation, the Van Buren Street Methodist Church donated two lots at 28th and Portland (Princeton). The mission congregants then purchased the Michigan Avenue Methodist Episcopal Church building for $1,500 and moved it from 32nd and Indiana to its Armour Square site. They renamed the edifice the Portland Avenue Methodist Church. On the occasion of its opening in 1870 the church had 13 members, two years later 70, and by 1884 just over 200.

The German Catholics of Armour Square, meanwhile, founded two separate parishes. St. Anthony's of Padua, located in Bridgeport, was opened in 1873. The founders of this institution originally had been members of the parish of St. Peter in the Loop but had left after the fire of 1871. Shortly after

The "men's gymnasium" in Armour Square Park, 1913. This halftone shows a portion of Armour Square Park, opened in 1904 north of Comiskey Park. It is typical of the small parks developed in working-class neighborhoods of Chicago after 1900. The park is now part of an informal boundary dividing white ethnics from blacks. From *Seeing Chicago by the Photograph Route*, CHS.

242–268 W. 26th Street, 1966. This is a very old block by Chicago standards: only the four-story apartment building and the adjacent single-story pizza shop were built after 1886. The block is now part of a triangle bordered on the south and east by the Dan Ryan Expressway and one of its ramps, and on the north by the Stevenson Expressway. Photo by Sigmund J. Osty, CHS.

the founding of St. Anthony's, a number of Bohemians became communicants. Eventually the Bohemians formed their own parish, St. John Nepomucene, originally located at 25th and Princeton but later moved to another building in Bridgeport. The second German Catholic parish in Armour Square was St. George's established at 39th and Wentworth in 1889.

The Irish, who were the second-largest ethnic group in Armour Square by the last quarter of the nineteenth century, did not form their own parish but attended All Saints Church in Bridgeport. All Saints had been founded in 1875, an offshoot of the older parishes of St. Bridget's and Nativity of Our Lord in Bridgeport and of St. James in Douglas. The Armour Square Irish also attended other Bridgeport churches as well as St. Cecilia's in Fuller Park, the neighborhood immediately to the south.

The Swedes followed the Germans and the Irish to Armour Square in the 1870s, settling first south of 16th Street and east of Clark. In 1868 almost half of the Swedes who lived on the South Side resided in this enclave. By 1870 they had joined those who had settled west of Clark, and within another year, the Swedish colony of about 500 began moving into Armour Square, primarily between 20th and 27th, Wentworth and Stewart. A decade later there would be around 1,300 Swedes between 22nd and 30th, west of Clark and east of Stewart.

While constituting only 7 percent of all their compatriots in Chicago and a minority among the other ethnic groups on the South Side and in Armour Square, the Swedes in this neighborhood were developing their own institutions. In 1868 they organized a Swedish Lutheran Congregation at Bushnell and 23rd streets. The Second Swedish Baptist Church was founded in 1874 and within

seven years the Methodists and the Mission Friends had organized congregations in the immediate area as well. Eventually, five Swedish churches were located in Armour Square, as were also the Svithoid Society, the Svenska Bibliotekssällakapet (Swedish Library Society), and the Scandinavian Society. But just as quickly as the Swedes had moved into Armour Square they moved out. The Swedish Methodists moved their church to 33rd and Fifth Avenue in the late 1870s, renaming it the Fifth Avenue Swedish Methodist Church. The Swedish Lutherans also migrated, taking the Salem Lutheran Church in 1885 to Princeton, between 28th and 29th, just down the block from the German Methodist Episcopal Church.

The movement of these various ethnic groups to and through Armour Square in the decades after 1860 is indicative of the character of this neighborhood of working-class families with the aspiration and ability to move upward on the socio-economic ladder. In coming to Armour Square they were making their first move from apartments into small houses. During the last two decades of the nineteenth century that movement was accelerating and, by 1895, all the building lots in the neighborhood were filled. The speed-up was associated with changes occurring at the edges of the community area. The establishment of new railroad trunk lines and the growth of the meat-packing industry brought more people into the area, as did the installation of various smaller plants along the railroad tracks on the eastern and western edges of the neighborhood.

At the beginning of the twentieth century industrial and commercial establishments began to enter Armour Square from the north. Some were of dubious character, extensions of the notorious First Ward Levee District. The coming of these "commercial"

establishments, plus the concurrent arrival of other more legitimate businesses, crowded out residential facilities. The neighborhood's mixed character was confirmed by the establishment of several baseball parks in and around Armour Square. In 1900 the Chicago White Sox played in a park at 39th (Pershing) and Wentworth. Just west of that park was a diamond where the Union Giants, a black team, played. Then, in 1908, Charles Comiskey bought fifteen acres from the estate of "Long John" Wentworth, paying $15,000 for the land which lay between 34th and 35th, Shields and Wentworth. This land was then an open field which had been used since the 1860s for various athletic events, including baseball games and bicycle races. The White Sox played their first game in this new park on April 15, 1910, although the facility was not dedicated until July 2, 1910. The black team, now renamed the American Giants, moved into the old Sox Park at 39th. Thus, at the end of the first decade of the twentieth century, two different teams had their home ground in Armour Square.

Meanwhile, two other physical changes affected the character of the neighborhood. In 1892 the New York Central tracks along the eastern boundary of the community area were elevated above grade, closing many of the streets between Armour Square and Douglas. In 1906 the same kind of elevation occurred to the west, when the tracks of the Pennsylvania and the Fort Wayne and Indiana railroads were raised, cutting off Armour Square's sister neighborhood of Bridgeport. By the first decade of the twentieth century, Armour Square was a narrow north-south chute. The housing stock of the area, now forty to fifty years old, deteriorated quickly as new groups swept through this narrow corridor.

Italians were moving into the neighborhood as the Sox were playing their first games there. In 1899, in a large apartment building known as "Il Pallazzone," a group of Southern Italians from Ricigliano in the Province of Salerno met and formed the group that became the parish of Santa Maria Incoronata. The first meeting place of this parish was a small chapel in St. John's School at 18th and Clark. St. John's parishioners were supportive of this new group of Catholics in other ways as well. One parishioner in particular, Mrs. Mollie O'Neill Cleary, assisted them by paying the rent on a new chapel at 21st and State when the St. John's chapel became too small for the group. In 1904 the Santa Maria Inconorata parish built its first church at 218 West Alexander, near Wentworth, in what was then the heart of the Italian community. Another Italian church, St. Michael's, located on 24th Place near Wentworth, was dedicated in 1903 and forty years later the parish of Santa Lucia opened a church building at 30th and Wells. The founding of the latter church indicated that the Italians, like other groups before them, were moving south through Armour Square. That trend continued in the years after World War II and in 1964 the decision was made to combine Santa Lucia with its mother church, Santa Maria Incoronata. The church of Santa Maria was then rededicated as St. Theresa's Chinese mission to serve the growing Catholic community of Chinatown.

Croatians also came to Armour Square after 1900, taking over the Swedish Salem Church at 28th and Princeton where they installed the parish of St. Jerome's in 1912. In 1939 this parish purchased a German Methodist Episcopal Church and converted it to a parish hall and social center.

Some years before the outbreak of World War I another group appeared in Armour Square. In 1912 the Chinese, who for the most part had lived in an enclave at the south edge of the Loop, moved en masse to the area surrounding the intersection of Cermak and Wentworth avenues. The shift involved a major real estate deal made through the H. O. Stone Company. In this transaction, about fifty Chinese businessmen assumed ten-year leases —totalling $50,000 in annual rents—on buildings in the new area, while a remnant of the old Chinese community remained on the Near South Side. The result was two rival Chinatowns, each dominated by a different group.

Chinese immigrants to America had brought with them fraternal associations or societies known as tongs, and these became important local communal organizations for Chinese in the New World. The South Loop area was dominated by the Hip Sing Tong while the Wentworth Avenue neighborhood was organized by the On Leong Tong. These two tongs had been involved in almost continuous warfare of one kind or another in China for some 3,000 years—a rivalry common among other tongs and manifested in tong warfare in cities all over the world. Chicago's Chinatown was generally peaceful, however, especially after the move to the Wentworth Avenue location, which was the home of Chin Kung Fong, a mediator in the war between the two tongs.

Today only a minority of the city's Chinese reside in Chinatown but many come back to the community to shop and worship. Standing as the symbolic center of Chinatown is the headquarters of the Chinese Merchants Association which is often called the Chinese City Hall. A more striking piece of oriental architecture than the Merchants Association building, however, is the ornamented tile gate which was constructed in 1975 to span Wentworth Avenue just south of Cermak Road (22nd Street). Based on traditional forms, this structure was designed by Peter Fung and constructed at a cost of $70,000. Inscribed with quotations from Sun Yat-Sen and Chiang Kai-Shek, this structure asserts the vitality of the Chinese community and its determination to remain in the inner city. The gate is only the most overt manifestation of an impressive rehabilitation effort based entirely on private investment in the area. Much of the new housing being erected around Chinatown was developed through the efforts of the Neighborhood Redevelopment Association, Inc. Other investors also are looking at Chinatown. One is Shiu Tam, a Hong Kong apparel magnate, who in August 1977 announced plans to construct a $10,000,000 condominium project at 24th and Canal. The project, to be called Appleville, is to consist of 132 two- and three-bedroom apartments.

Blacks began to move into Armour Square during World War I. They came from the east, as the black belt broadened and lengthened between 1915 and 1920. In the latter year, blacks accounted for 23 percent of the neighborhood's population of 21,450. That figure declined during the next decade to 18.9 percent. In the depression decade the total population dropped to 18,472, with blacks constituting 22 percent of this total. There were no major additions to the housing stock between 1910 and 1940 but old houses were converted into small apartments and overcrowding increased.

In the 1940s Armour Square began to experience the effect of policy changes implemented from outside the neighborhood. In 1947 the Chicago Housing Authority completed Wentworth Gardens at 37th and Princeton. This federally financed project contained twenty-eight two-story and nine three-story buildings on sixteen acres at the southernmost part of the community. Altogether, Wentworth Gardens had 422 units which were occupied almost entirely by blacks. The public housing program added less than 40 percent of the new units opened in Armour Square during the 1940s, however. The remainder were created through conversion of old apartments into smaller units. The result was reflected in the 1950 census. Through the previous decade, the population of the neighborhood increased by 26.1 percent to reach an all-time high of 23,294. Blacks made up 46.9 percent of the total population.

The developmental history of Armour Square changed radically in the 1950s as demolition began for the Dan Ryan Expressway which ran north and south through the community along its eastern edge between Pershing Road and 28th, where it swung northwest across the corridor neighborhood. Preparations for the Stevenson Expressway entailed taking out another strip of buildings, this one running east and west along 25th. This demolition was mirrored in the housing figures. Between 1950 and 1960 the number of dwelling units in Armour Square declined by 1,435 to a total of 4,492. The only new construction offsetting the losses due to the construction of the expressway was the 1952 installation by the Chicago Housing Authority of Archer Courts, 147 units in two seven-story buildings. This city–state financed construction occupied only a little more than four acres at 23rd and Princeton, just west of Chinatown. The 1960 population of the neighborhood reflected the dramatic drop in housing stock, with the census showing only 15,783 inhabitants, down 32.4 percent from a decade earlier. The demolition also had lowered the percentage of blacks in the neighborhood to 31.4 percent in 1960.

The Chicago Housing Authority continued to be the most important builder of new dwelling units in Armour Square through the 1960s. In 1965 a federally sponsored project for the elderly, the 198-unit Armour Square Apartments, located at 3146–3216 South Wentworth, was opened. This project consisted of two 13-story apartment buildings on 3.59 acres of land. Two years earlier, the Housing Authority had opened the Raymond Hilliard Homes on seven acres of land at 22nd and State, just east of Chinatown. This project was remarkable only in that it was designed by Bertrand Goldberg, who had been the architect for the Marina Towers located on the main stem of the Chicago River in the north Loop. The design for the Hilliard Homes was a stark, stripped-down version of the Marina plans, demonstrating what happens when a design is held to the strict cost standards maintained for federally financed public housing projects.

By 1970 the effect of public housing on Armour Square was demonstrated by the fact that 33.5 percent of all dwelling units there had been erected during the preceding thirty years. The neighborhood population, meanwhile, had dropped to 13,060. Blacks constituted 31.8 percent of the total, less than a 1 percent change over a decade. Spanish-speaking groups had also made their appearance in the district and made up 6.1 percent of the total population in 1970.

Armour Square today is a community in name only. Actually, it is a set of at least three enclaves. The Chinese, the principal ethnic group in the area, live mainly in the few blocks north and south of Cermak Road. Blacks are concentrated in a small ghetto mainly south of 35th Street. Italians, Croatians, and Spanish occupy much of the space in the middle of the area, bounded on the south by Comiskey Park and on the north by the Ryan and Stevenson expressways. There were no foreign-born Swedes in the area in 1970 and only 41 Irish and German-born combined. While the population groups in the area are quite diverse they share two characteristics. First, the median number of school years completed by neighborhood adults was only 8.9, which is very low compared to figures for the surrounding neighborhoods and the city as a whole. Associated with this low educational level was low income: in 1970, 60 percent of all families in Armour Square earned under $10,000 and 23.2 percent earned under $5,000.

No single policy will suffice to deal with the problems that remain in Armour Square: the disparities within the community area are too great. The Chinese and Italian district at the north end of the neighborhood area seems to have the best prospects. If local leaders continue to attract outside investors, the resurgence of this section should continue. The public housing already constructed in the southern half of the neighborhood has not provided sufficient stimulus for further improvement there and most of the dwelling units are old and badly worn. Comiskey Park, meanwhile, shows its age to all but the most avid White Sox fans who glory in its history. Because Armour Square is a set of enclaves, its future is tied both to continued private investment and to public policies on demolition, renewal, and public housing. That future would also be affected by the development of a new sports complex for Chicago which is presently under consideration.

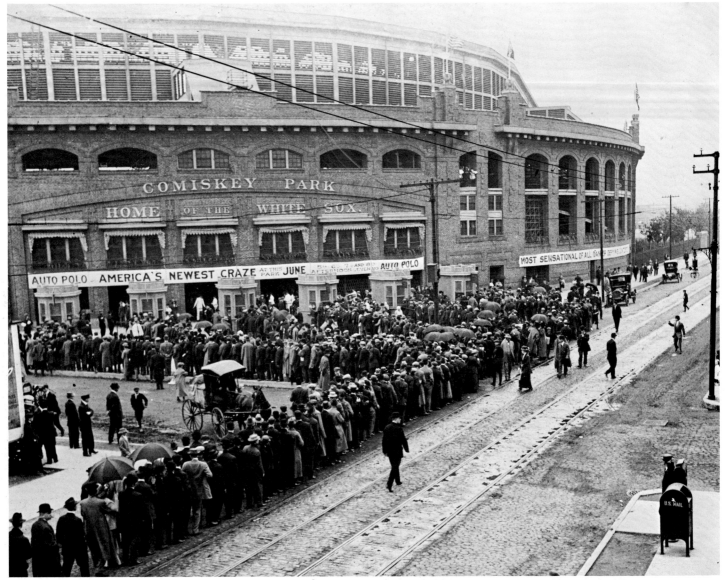

Comiskey Park, view from 35th Street looking northwest along Wentworth Avenue, 1913. As the banner above the entrance to the park attests, baseball was not the only sports event held here in the early years. Completed in 1910, Comiskey Park is the oldest professional baseball field used by the major leagues. CHS.

St. Jerome's Church, 2823 S. Princeton Avenue, 1954. Having formed a parish in 1912, the Croatians bought this structure, designed by Christian O. Hansen, from a Swedish congregation. Photo courtesy of *The Chicago Catholic* (formerly *The New World*).

Parade on Wentworth Avenue in Chinatown, 1972. Around 3,000 Chinese live in Armour Square and many more are drawn to the neighborhood by cultural events like this one. Photo by Casey Prunchunas, CHS.

Part of the Wentworth Gardens project, 3770 S. Wentworth Avenue, 1954. The Federal Public Housing Authority completed this project in 1947 on the site where the Chicago White Sox and later the Negro League's Chicago Giants once played. The development, designed by architects Loebl and Schlossman, consists of three-story apartment buildings surrounded by two-story row homes like this one. The Chicago Housing Authority took over ownership of the project in 1956. Photo by Mildred Mead, CHS.

Archer Courts Housing project, 23rd Street and Archer Avenue, 1952. The project, designed by architects Everett F. Quinn and Alfred Mell, consists entirely of three-bedroom apartments. Photo by Mildred Mead, CHS.

View northeast across the Dan Ryan Expressway, 1969. The multiple towers of the Robert Taylor Homes, and the neighborhoods of the Near South Side, Douglas, and Armour Square are visible on the right. The Dan Ryan Expressway reinforced a "natural" South Side neighborhood boundary; its eight express lanes, six regular lanes, and entrance and exit ramps added a full block of width to the Rock Island Railroad tracks which already acted as a major dividing line. The single tower of the Illinois Institute of Technology is visible at the center of the photograph near the top. CHS.

BRIDGEPORT

Bridgeport, one of Chicago's oldest neighborhoods, is located about five miles southwest of the Loop on the South Branch of the Chicago River. This community area is perhaps best known because it includes the 11th Ward, often called the political capital of Chicago. All four of Chicago's mayors since 1932 have come from Bridgeport. Indeed, though politics is not the only profession practiced in Bridgeport, it is certainly one of the most important. In 1970, for example, 12.8 percent of the employed persons in the community worked at government jobs. Local government was the largest public employer, accounting for 12.2 percent of all male employment and 9.8 percent of all female employment. And, while these figures are impressive, they do not tell the full story, for the Democratic Party organization also has considerable ability to obtain private industry jobs for its loyal supporters.

Bridgeport originally was settled in the 1830s by Irish laborers who came to help construct the Illinois-Michigan Canal. The homes of these early residents were wooden shanties strung along the banks of the South Branch of the Chicago River. Because the panic of 1837 held up construction on the canal, the population of Bridgeport remained small until after 1842. When work on the canal resumed, population increased rapidly. It was during the 1840s that the neighborhood acquired its name. A low bridge was constructed over the South Branch at Ashland Avenue and heavily-laden barges carrying goods to Chicago from the southwest had to stop at this bridge to unload. The place at which the barge traffic stopped became a "port" and the area acquired the name Bridgeport.

When the canal was completed in 1848, canal-related industry moved to Bridgeport and the availability of jobs attracted more newcomers, notably Irish immigrants fleeing the great potato famine in their homeland. The chief industry to locate in the area was meat slaughtering. Initially, slaughterhouses had been located along the North Branch of the Chicago River near the center of the city. As the retail and wholesale functions of the central area expanded and required more space, the packers were forced to relocate. Bridgeport provided an excellent alternative site for their operations. Not only was there a ready supply of water for use in the slaughtering process and a stream in which to dump offal, but Archer Avenue, named for Colonel William Archer, the best-known engineer of the canal project, ran southwest to Joliet. Herders drove their animals up Archer to the city's packinghouses until the 1880s. Along this road that paralleled both the canal and the Chicago River, stores, taverns, and hotels sprang up to serve the cattle herders and other travelers who arrived from the southwest.

The best known of the early stockyards serving the packers in the Bridgeport area was the Brighton Yards, established in the 1840s, at the corner of Archer and 39th (also Egan Avenue, and later Pershing Road). There were numerous other yards scattered throughout the South Side, however. The consolidation of several of these yards into the Union Stock Yard in 1865 had enormous impact on Bridgeport, for when the consolidation occurred, the independent packers relocated just west of the yards. Improved railroad facilities played an important role in this relocation because the combined stockyards and packers were becoming increasingly dependent on rail transportation. As a consequence, the cattle drives down Archer Avenue came to an end leaving the street to become a travel corridor in and out of the Loop. Archer Avenue's present mixed character derives in part from its former role as the "main drag" for the great drives and in part from its subsequent role as a residual street along which tenements and stores competed for space.

Internal transportation also improved during the 1880s and 1890s. Prior to the fire of 1871 Bridgeport was not well served by public transportation, and most workers without the financial means to travel any other way walked to work in the stockyards and factories of Bridgeport and nearby areas. Still, enough people used mass transit to stimulate the development of a business district at the streetcar intersection of 35th and Halsted. This district never became very large, however. First, it was overshadowed by two other business sections: one at 47th and Ashland in the Back of the Yards, and the other just a short streetcar ride away at 63rd and Halsted in Englewood. Second, both 35th and Halsted were strip commercial streets, and the string of shops, saloons, and offices lining them detracted from the development of the intersection.

Other basic urban services like water and sewers remained at a low level, in spite of the fact that the entire area was annexed to the city of Chicago in 1863. The reasons for this were quite simple: the area was new and its inhabitants were both poor and politically unorganized. Therefore, the neighborhood did not have the power to obtain those services which were badly needed.

While Bridgeport originally was settled by the Irish they soon were joined by other groups. First a few native Americans, then Germans came to work in the stockyards and the packing plants in the early 1860s.

Many of these Germans were skilled butchers and moved quickly into the higher paying jobs in the packing plants. Bridgeport's ethnic diversity increased in the 1880s and 1890s with the arrival of Eastern Europeans. During those two decades, breweries, brickyards, and steel mills moved into the neighborhood. Attracted by the new job opportunities offered by these manufacturing establishments as well as by the continuing expansion of the packing plants, Slavic groups moved to Bridgeport in large numbers. Poles and Lithuanians, who came from neighboring regions in Europe, became neighbors in the stockyards area, settling mainly in the northwestern section of the community near the river. Morgan Street, the major thoroughfare there, became a boundary between the two communities, with Lithuanians living to the east and Poles to the west of the street.

The churches of Bridgeport reflect the ethnic diversity of the area. In 1846 the Irish organized the parish of St. Bridget on Archer Avenue. The German presence was manifested in the organization of the First Lutheran Church of the Trinity, built on 25th Place and Canal Street in 1863. This congregation relocated in a new building at 31st and Lowe in 1913. An offshoot of Trinity, Holy Cross Lutheran Church, to be found in the 3100 block of Racine, still conducts its Sunday services in German. Before the second great wave of immigration from eastern Europe ended with World War I, Poles had organized two Catholic parishes, St. Mary of Perpetual Help in 1882 and St. Barbara's in 1910. The Lithuanians, meanwhile, established St. George's on Lituanica Street in 1892. These churches were important not only because they served the spiritual needs of their members but also because they established parochial

schools which neighborhood residents often preferred to the public schools. The parochial school tradition remains strong in Bridgeport, as it does in all the old ethnic working-class neighborhoods.

Thus, at the time that Bridgeport reached residential maturity, the church was the central institution of the community. It provided weekly or daily religious services for the faithful and the traditional rites of passage—baptism, marriage, and funeral services—for the not-so-faithful. Meanwhile, the church-sponsored schools, in addition to offering instruction in the usual academic subjects and religion, maintained in varying degrees the ethnic traditions of the predominant group in the parish.

If the church was one important ethnic neighborhood institution, the saloon was another. Since the homes of most working-class families were crowded, the tavern offered an important social meeting place and a forum for the discussion of all topics—especially politics. Such drinking establishments were scattered throughout the ward, with those on the side streets catering to members of one or another ethnic group, while those on the main business streets often provided a meeting place for mixed groups. The most "political" tavern in Bridgeport is Schaller's Pump on the corner of 37th and Halsted, directly across from 11th Ward Regular Democratic Organization headquarters.

Such political associations were only one of the numerous symbiotic relationships which made up the essence of community in a working-class ethnic neighborhood. The saloon keeper also fulfilled some other functions in the neighborhood. In hard times he might become the confessor, banker, savings and loan director, and neighborhood philosopher, as well as carrying out his

Deering Street Police Station, Archer Avenue and Deering Street, 1872. Originally known as the South Branch Sub-Station of the First Precinct, this police station, established in 1871, was manned by a sergeant and sixteen patrolmen charged with keeping the peace in Bridgeport. Initially located on Deering Street (now Loomis), it was the forerunner of the present Deering District Station at 35th and Lowe. CHS.

De La Salle Institute, 35th Street and Wabash Avenue, ca. 1890. Founded by Brother Adjutor of Mary and operated by the Christian Brothers, the school is housed in this building erected between 1889 and 1892. Although located in the Douglas community area, De La Salle has educated many of Bridgeport's best-known sons, including Mayor Richard J. Daley. The tower shown in this engraving was never constructed. CHS.

regular role as political organizer. His tavern often provided a place for union members to gather before they had the means to build their own union hall. Even the public school eventually acquired a place in the fabric of community relationships. Initially viewed as a hostile institution by the Irish immigrants, the public school came to be accepted by many families because it offered several benefits. First, it provided the children of the working class with the education to move away from manual labor to more prestigious and higher paying occupations. Second, it offered custodial care for the sons and daughters of working women, keeping the children off the streets. Such benefits often outweighed the parents' fear that their children might pick up ideas threatening to the values of their imported culture.

Emphasis on communalism was a strong characteristic of Bridgeport history during the latter part of the nineteenth century and has continued to be so ever since. The geographic neighborhood, as it has been interpreted by the residents of this area, has continually faced problems which have had to be dealt with by groups rather than individuals. Inadequate housing, poverty, and labor problems have led Bridgeport residents to seek remedies through the communal network of the local Democratic machine on the one hand and through the offices of organized labor on the other. In Bridgeport, as in other working-class neighborhoods, these institutions reinforced each other precisely because they were based in the community and in familial relationships.

Such extended and overlapping relationships were particularly apparent in the Hamburg section of Bridgeport. This area, bounded on the north by 35th, on the south by 39th, on the west by Halsted, and on the east by the Penn Central railroad tracks, continues to be predominantly Irish. But like all old immigrant areas it has never been exclusively inhabited by one group. So strong were the social and spatial associations in enclaves like Hamburg that they resembled small self-contained villages located in the midst of a large city. And through the hierarchical parish structure, social and political organizations, and kinship, each such village was linked to other similar places throughout the city. The strength of such affiliative structures cannot be overestimated. This set of linkages continues to provide the basis for neighborhood organizations, labor unions, and political parties.

It is appropriate to pay particular attention to the Hamburg section of Bridgeport because, for the past quarter century it has received national attention. Chicago's former mayor, Richard J. Daley, was born and raised in this area and spent most of his private and much of his public life there. Daley received his political start as a member of the Hamburgs, one of Chicago's youth gangs which eventually developed into a political organization under the trappings of a social athletic club. Not only was Daley a member of the Hamburgs, but his

Phillip Koch's Shoe Store, 3011 S. Archer Avenue, ca. 1882. Finley Peter Dunne, creator of Mr. Dooley, made Archer Avenue famous for its taverns, but it also had many stores like this one because it was the main shopping district for old Bridgeport as well as the spiritual heart of the community. From the Joseph Ryerson collection, CHS.

accomplishments as a leader of the club foreshadowed his later success as a political figure in Bridgeport and Chicago. Hamburg returned his loyalty. Under his leadership and that of his successor, Mayor Michael A. Bilandic, also an 11th Ward regular, Hamburg has been the most loyal section of a loyal Bridgeport in turning out votes for the Democratic organization.

In 1920 Bridgeport had a population of 60,443, with 36 percent of that total foreign born. Since then the neighborhood has grown both older and younger while losing population in the process. One reason that the Bridgeport population has grown older is the emigration of the sons and daughters of older residents. Thus, the percentage of the population between the ages of 20 and 44 years of age has declined from 34.4 percent in 1930 to 26.0 percent of a total of 41,560 in 1960. During the same period the percentage of those 65 years and older has risen from 3.3 to 9.4

The 1970 census shows an extremely high 62.3 percent of a total of 35,231 residing in the same house in which they had lived five years earlier, indicating a large stable element in the population. Between 1930 and 1960, the portion of the population under the age of five rose from 8.5 to 11.1 percent, and in the last decade that percentage has increased dramatically. The main immigration bringing this change is the arrival of Mexican-Americans. In 1930 Poles, Lithuanians, and Italians were the leading groups of foreign born. In 1970 the Poles still led, accounting for 26.9 percent of all foreign-born residents in the community. The Mexican group, however, was now second, amounting to 21.1 percent of the total. The Lithuanians and the Italians were close behind. Blacks accounted for only 3.5 percent of the total neighborhood population, up from one-tenth of one percent in 1960.

The absolute decline in total population, amounting to a loss of 25,212—or 41.7 percent—between 1930 and 1970 can be explained by the industrial and transport pressures exerted on Bridgeport. While almost no new housing has been constructed in the neighborhood since 1920, there has been considerable industrial development. The Central Manufacturing District expanded between 1920 and 1930, displacing some housing units. New industrial plants were also installed in the area bounded by the South Fork, 31st Street, and Racine Avenue, along the Chicago and Alton Railroad. Finally, the building of the Stevenson Expressway in the 1960s forced demolition of another large section of housing. Industry and transportation, which first brought the Irish to Bridgeport, have led to a decline in the area's population during the past forty years.

The 1970 census shows that families earning between $10,000 and $15,000 predominate in Bridgeport, indicating that the essential working-class character of the neighborhood has remained intact.

James Jesse's Saloon, 3801 S. Halsted Street, ca. 1881. Thomas Jesse opened a saloon at this corner in 1880. This establishment and others near it were within easy walking distance of the 41st Street entrance to the stockyards. From the Joseph Ryerson collection, CHS.

St. Bridget's Catholic Church, 2928–2954 S. Archer Avenue, 1961. The congregation of this church, organized in 1847 as a mission of St. Patrick's Church, celebrated mass at the homes of various parishioners until a permanent chapel was built in 1850. The cornerstone of the present church was laid on September 17, 1905, replacing an older structure that had been erected in 1855. Photo by Betty Hulett, CHS.

Southwest corner of 35th and Halsted streets, 1970. This corner, which has served several generations of Bridgeport businesses, was originally a good commercial location because of its proximity to several mass transit lines. Now the home of a restaurant, this building is a good example of saloon architecture, but the large second- and third-floor apartment space, built in the belief that the corner would grow into a large shopping district, is atypical of the neighborhood. Photo by Sigmund J. Osty, CHS.

Thirty-sixth Street looking west from Lituanica Avenue, 1971. Bridgeport has streets lined with brick as well as wooden residences, although the size of lots and the living space remain relatively small. In the background is the Spiegel Warehouse in the Central Manufacturing District. The street name, Lituanica, reflects the presence of a large Lithuanian population in Bridgeport; St. George's Lithuanian Catholic Church is only a short walk from this corner. Photo by Casey Prunchunas, CHS.

The north end of Bridgeport, 1969. Construction of an interchange for the Dan Ryan Expressway (in the lower left of the photograph) and the Stevenson Expressway was a major reason for a dramatic population drop in the area between 1960 and 1970. Near the upper left of the picture, the Stevenson begins to run parallel to the Illinois and Michigan Canal along the old Chicago portage route. It was this route which provided the impetus for the first settlement of the city. CHS.

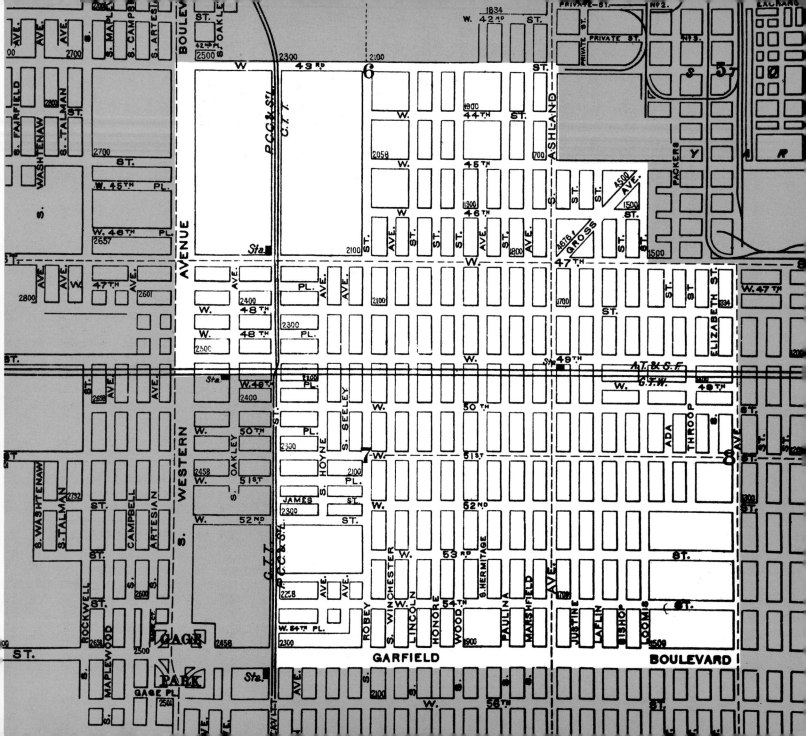

BACK OF THE YARDS

When Chicago sociologists were laying out formal community area boundaries in the 1920s they saw the areas east and west of the Union Stock Yard as one entity. They named this large expanse New City. That name had historic roots. Real estate dealer and builder S. E. Gross, who began to develop a number of subdivisions around 47th and Ashland in the 1880s, applied the title New City to one of his developments. After that, however, it fell out of common usage, only to be misapplied to a much larger and quite artificial community area many decades later. Actually, at least two separate communities exist inside the formal boundaries of New City—Back of the Yards and Canaryville—and they have quite separate histories.

The Back of the Yards was first settled in the late 1860s and early 1870s. The name of the neighborhood reveals the reason for its existence—it is located south and west of the Union Stock Yard. The original settlers were predominantly Irish immigrants and some Germans who worked in the yards or the packing plants that were built just west of the ramps and pens. The first homes for these workers were small cottages clustered near the corner of 43rd and Loomis Street. As the industry expanded westward in the 1880s these houses were torn down and new ones were erected farther southwest. A growing population in an expanding country needed meat and Chicago was ideally situated to provide it. The most obvious neighborhood manifestation of this growing industry was Back of the Yards.

By the 1890s the neighborhood began to attract the new immigrants arriving from southern and eastern Europe. Slavs, the majority of whom were Poles, were the largest new group to come to work in the district. The first Polish family, named Zulawski, came to the Back of the Yards in 1877, but their compatriots did not arrive in significant numbers until after the packinghouse strike of 1886. The newcomers moved into wooden tenement houses on the western and southern edges of the yards. Other Slavic groups followed them. By 1920 the New City area as a whole recorded a population of 92,659. Of these 37 percent were foreign born, with Poles, Irish, Czechoslovakians, Germans, and Lithuanians constituting the chief groups who lived there. Although these figures encompassed more than just the Back of the Yards, they generally reflect the pattern in that neighborhood.

Mexicans began to arrive in Back of the Yards during World War I and continued to settle there during the 1920s. This was the last major influx of a new nationality into the Back of the Yards. The 1970 census figures confirm the continuity of a decades-old trend. Of all persons listed as foreign-born in New City, the two largest groups were Poles, 35.4 percent, and Mexicans, 24.7 percent. Blacks, meanwhile, constituted only 3.5 percent of the total population of New City.

Ethnicity was manifested throughout the history of Back of the Yards in the character of its churches. The Irish established St. Rose of Lima in 1881 on Ashland and 48th. The Germans opened the St. Martini Lutheran Church in 1884 and the St. Augustine Roman Catholic Church in 1879. The first Poles in the community attended services at St. Adalbert's Catholic parish in the Pilsen neighborhood four miles to the north. The Poles established their own Catholic parish, St. Joseph's, in 1889. As the number of Poles in the area grew, two other Polish parishes were sanctioned by the Chicago Archdiocese, St. John of God opened in 1907 and Sacred Heart of Jesus in 1910. The numerical domination of Back of the Yards by the newer immigrants was quite apparent by the mid-1920s. Out of eleven Roman Catholic parishes in the district, seven were Slavic and one was Lithuanian. The relatively small Jewish community which established itself along Ashland Avenue in the first decades of the twentieth century organized a synagogue which remained in existence until World War II, while the Poles formed a parish of the Polish National Catholic Church in the same area. Like earlier ethnic groups, the Mexicans established their own place of worship in the Immaculate Heart of Mary parish on the 4500 block of South Ashland Avenue. Unlike the earlier groups, however, the Mexicans did not organize a parish school, instead their children attended the various parochial and public schools already established in the neighborhood.

From the beginning, housing conditions were a problem in this neighborhood. The rapid growth of the work force in the yards during the latter half of the nineteenth century and the relatively low pay (combined with a lack of adequate transportation) meant that workers had to live in what was already there. The characteristic house in this nineteenth century neighborhood was the Chicago balloon frame. The most typical housing unit—still to be found on the side streets of the neighborhood—was the "double-decker." These two-story structures were built in almost identical style, the only variation being in the treatment of entrances and stairways. House lots were small, usually with a 25-foot front, so that the maximum width of the house was only 22 to 23 feet, leaving room for a gangway on one side of the lot by which a back yard could be reached. The business streets were lined with tenements. Two or three stories high,

usually with one window to a room, these tenements were occupied not only by single workers but often by whole families, who crowded into them to save on rent or, if times were good, to put away money so that they could eventually buy a house. As a result, housing conditions in Back of the Yards were so bad that a 1901 survey of Chicago housing failed to include the neighborhood because of its atypicality. The construction of a few brick houses and small flat buildings west of Ashland and south of 49th in the 1890s only pointed up more vividly the inadequacies of the remainder of the neighborhood's housing.

The smoke-belching and smelly meat-packing plants dominated the texture of life in Back of the Yards until the mid-twentieth century. After the Union Stock Yard opened in 1865, the packers quickly moved in. Armour and Company opened a large plant there in 1867 and the other meat companies followed. By 1884 there were thirty companies in Packingtown. Also, after 1870, by-product plants which converted hooves into glue and tallow into lard were opened up by the packers. Other "dirty" industrial and warehousing industries moved into Packingtown, including coal and lumber yards. It was the visits he paid to Packingtown and Back of the Yards that prompted Upton Sinclair to write his famous muckraking novel, *The Jungle*, in 1905. While Sinclair tended to exaggerate the problems faced by the immigrants, he captured the essence of working-class life in the area before World War I.

The conditions were little eased by city government. Not until a decade after the area's annexation to Chicago in 1889 were even a few streets paved. This small accomplishment came at the same time that a horsecar line was first installed on 47th

Street to a western terminal at Ashland Avenue. Still, even by the turn of the century, the Back of the Yards had few sewers, no electric lights, and, for many householders, an inadequate water suply.

Because of low wages and poor housing, Back of the Yards residents were faced with two serious problems: bad health and juvenile delinquency. Through the first third of the twentieth century, this district's death rate from tuberculosis was one of the highest in the city. The death rate for children under five was particularly high, especially along the streets that ran parallel with the old city dumps. These were located in the open fields along 47th Street between Robey (now Damen) and Western until World War I. The odors from these dumps, combined with those from Bubbly Creek (the stem of the South Branch of the Chicago River that ran through Packingtown), and those which were part of the packing process itself, gave the neighborhood its most notorious symbol.

The juvenile delinquency problem stemmed from the youth gangs. The area around 43rd and Ashland was especially known for gang activities during the late nineteenth century and it was understood by all the area's inhabitants that certain ethnically oriented gangs would fight for their right to dominate their particular section of the community. Gangs, however, do not appear to have been as important in the Back of the Yards as they were in the area that bordered the black belt east of Wentworth Avenue.

Those who have studied the history of Chicago communities give 1914 as the year in which New City reached residential maturity. Its population peak of 92,659, as measured by the census, was reached six years later. Thereafter, the population of the neighborhood has shown a steady numerical decline. Between 1920 and 1940 it drop-

THE WORKING MAN'S REWARD.

WHERE ALL WAS DARKNESS, NOW IS LIGHT.

A HOME AT $10.00 A MONTH

S. E. GROSS'
ASHLAND AVE. AND 47TH STREET SUBDIVISION
BRANCH OFFICE COR. ASHLAND AVE & 47TH ST.

South-east corner Dearborn and Randolph Sts.

A HOME FOR $100
In my Ashland Avenue and 47th Street Subdivision.

LOCATION:

These handsome cottages are located on 45th St. and Laflin St., between 45th and 46th Sts., (see plat of property on page 61)

FIRST FLOOR.

BASEMENT.

DESCRIPTION.

They are well built and thoroughly finished throughout. Have seven foot basement, lake water, sewers and large lot. Sidewalks laid and fences built.

TERMS.

Price $1,050 to $1,500; $100 cash, balance on long time and monthly payments of $9 to $11, same as rent.

BRANCH OFFICE AND HOW TO GET THERE.

Branch Office corner of 47th St. and Ashland Ave. Open every day. Take Archer and Ashland Aves. cars, or Halsted and 47th Sts. cars; either will take you to the office door; or take Grand Trunk R. R. trains to Ashland Ave. station and go two blocks north; or call at Main Office and you will be taken free to see the property.

South-east corner Dearborn and Randolph Sts.

Advertisement for a working-class cottage in Back of the Yards, 1891. Samuel E. Gross's 47th Street subdivision extended from 45th to 47th and from Laflin to Ashland. Gross built single-family cottages and also sold lots in his subdivision on which multiple-unit houses were later built. From *Tenth Annual Illustrated Catalog of S. E. Gross' Famous City Subdivisions and Suburban Towns*, CHS.

ped by more than 12,000. It was not until the late 1930s, however, that the community gathered sufficient strength to organize in an attempt to solve its own problems. In 1939, social activist Saul Alinsky, local leader Joseph Meegan, and Roman Catholic Bishop Bernard J. Sheil began to organize the community. The result was the Back of the Yards Neighborhood Council, important not only for what it soon did for the neighborhood, but also because it was Alinsky's first attempt at community organization. He went on to use the Yards model to form similar organizations in other parts of the country. The Neighborhood Council was organized with the cooperation of local businesses, churches, and the C.I.O. United Packinghouse Workers. This support from labor was especially significant and was reciprocated by the council when the union organized packinghouse workers in the late 1930s and early 1940s.

The Neighborhood Council attacked the delinquency problem by developing a number of organized activities for teenagers in neighborhood parks, schools, and at the University of Chicago Settlement House (which operated in the neighborhood from 1895 until 1975). The coordination of recreational activities and the development of good lines of communication between the Neighborhood Council and government authorities representing the Park District, school system, and police helped to cut dramatically the rate of juvenile delinquency. But while the work of the council was important, the New City area youth problem also diminished because of a reduction in the number of juveniles residing in the community. In 1930, 43.7 percent of all the New City population was aged 18 and under; by 1970 that figure was down to 34.4 percent.

The council also worked on housing pro-blems, obtaining assistance from the city, state, and federal governments to remodel older units. But there was little new construction. Of all housing units in New City in 1970, only 4.3 percent were constructed after 1940. Moreover, 60.1 percent were renter-occupied and only 37.5 percent were occupied by their owners. The predominant rental unit was in a two- to nine-unit building. Thus, the housing character of Back of the Yards established in the 1910s survived intact into the 1970s.

Eventually, the Neighborhood Council also encountered other problems. Critics saw it as changing from a progressive force for neighborhood rehabilitation into a reactonary organization which had as its primary purpose the maintenance of racial segregation. The council remains an important factor in the community's life, however, continuing to carry forward the purposes for which it was established: to help articulate community goals, to organize political support to get things done, and, when necessary, to veto unwanted changes. The very fact that it still arouses controversy shows that it remains a vital force in the life of the area.

The success of the Neighborhood Council and the relative stability of Back of the Yards is impressive because, historically, neighborhoods like this have been the most vulnerable to the pressure of deterioration and racial change.

The Back of the Yards has maintained its working-class character in spite of the decline of jobs available in the immediate area. In New City 86.2 percent of the male labor force worked for private corporations in 1970; 84 percent of all families in the area made less than $15,000 per year. The mean value of owner-occupied units was $13,776, compared with the city-wide measure of $22,752, while the mean contract rent was only $70, compared with the city-wide figure of $115.

As these statistics indicate, the families of Back of the Yards do not have large financial resources with which to work. Such a condition makes community organization all the more important if the neighborhood is to avoid what has become the usual fate of inner city areas—a massive tear-down. But whether the community can go beyond this defensive stance and actually renew itself remains to be seen. What happens to housing stock will be the best indicator of what lies ahead. Board-ups have increased over the past few years. If worn-out units are replaced by newer units constructed on the same sites and these units attract new residents and hold others in the neighborhood, then the work of Saul Alinsky and Joseph Meegan may come to be seen as more than a simple holding action. It may, indeed, come to be regarded as the necessary first step in neighborhood conservation and revitalization.

The business heart of Back of the Yards was and is 47th and Ashland. Here the typical building is a one- or two-story "store front." Although initially many of these structures were wooden, most are now made of brick or brick facing applied to cement blocks. Basically, this major retail area has changed little since the turn of the century, when this corner was the terminus for both the 47th Street and Ashland Avenue streetcar lines. The architectural character of the shopping streets is not particularly distinctive; only Goldblatt's Department Store at the southwest corner of Ashland and 47th shows any evidence of having been designed by an architect.

Along 47th west to the southern end of the Damen Avenue overpass and east to Loomis, can be found numerous ethnic

William Chambers's saloon and boarding house, 4109 S. Ashland Avenue, 1883. Boarding houses, many catering to particular ethnic groups, played an important role in the development of Back of the Yards. They provided single men with a place to socialize as well as a place to live. From the Joseph Ryerson collection, CHS.

stores, funeral parlors, restaurants, and taverns. Such establishments also radiate north and south from the intersection between 42nd and 51st. Taverns are especially prevalent in the 4200 through the 4500 block on Ashland. These drinking establishments originally were built as close as possible to the 43rd Street entrance to the stockyards, one of the main routes to and from work in Packingtown. Some of these taverns have taken on an ethnic flavor in recent years, a character that was not apparent early in the century when such establishments served a multi-ethnic workforce.

McDowell Avenue, which intersects 47th at Ashland, also played a complex role in the life of Back of the Yards residents. The street, formerly Gross Avenue, is named for Mary McDowell, the first head resident of the area's University of Chicago Settlement House. McDowell not only conducted the usual settlement activities but was also a strong supporter of union organization and the women's movement. At the intersection of McDowell, Laflin, and 46th is Whiskey Point, so called because each of the six corners of this intersection sported a saloon, while more drinking establishments radiated out along each street. Eventually, two of these corners were taken over by the Guardian Angel Nursery and Home for Working Women. Guardian Angel was established in 1913 by the three Polish parishes in Back of the Yards to act as an *ochronka* or shelter. In fact, the institution functioned as a settlement house which served all the ethnic groups residing in the neighborhood.

Mary McDowell is associated with one other important part of Back of the Yards, namely Davis Square Park. This was established in 1904 in response to agitation by Mary McDowell and her co-workers. Bounded by 44th and 45th, Marshfield and Hermitage, Davis Square was one of a number of little parks laid during the first decade and a half of the twentieth century as reformers came to recognize the importance of even small open spaces in the cramped working-class neighborhoods. The Davis Square Field House provided the local residents with both a boys' and a girls' gym, a swimming pool, library, meeting and game rooms, and showers. While the square has since served primarily as a neighborhood recreational facility, it also functioned as a place for mass meetings of workers when they were attempting to organize the packing industry. On December 8, 1921, the little square became the scene of a riot which started when mounted patrolmen and then motorcycle police tried to disperse the large group which had gathered in the park. Once the riot began the whole neighborhood joined in. Groups of women and children attacked the predominantly Irish policemen and usually respectable store keepers and venerated elders of the Polish community ended up among those arrested.

Back of the Yards has been one of a number of Chicago's receiver neighborhoods for the foreign born. In addition to being staging areas for upward mobility, such neighborhoods have also fostered a strong sense of identity among their residents, both past and present. Like Bridgeport, this part of the Stock Yard district promotes the same kind of relationships among its residents as are found in small towns. Such strong identities contribute to the success of organizations like the Back of the Yards Neighborhood Council.

The ethnics who lived in the Back of the Yards moved out in three different directions. Their first movement was southeast into Grand Boulevard and Washington Park, where they mixed with earlier residents. Others moved directly west on 43rd and 47th streets to Brighton Park and southwest into the Gage Park and Marquette Park neighborhoods. The three latter neighborhoods have experienced a large increase in the number of Slavic American inhabitants over recent decades as such groups abandoned the Back of the Yards for newer housing. Nevertheless, many of those who have left have maintained the primary relationships they made while living in Back of the Yards. A recent reunion of the graduating classes of the parochial school of the Sacred Heart Church brought together over a thousand people—not just from the immediate Chicago area but from all over the country. This meeting was only one overt sign that former Back of the Yards residents had not given up their old ethnic community ties.

St. Michael the Archangel, 48th and Damen, 1953. The church was founded in 1898 by the Slovak Catholic Society with the approval of Chicago Archbishop John Quigley and the help of the First Slovak Union. Its parochial school opened in 1902. The cornerstone of the present combination church-school building was laid on September 6, 1908. Photo by Arthur M. Weiland, CHS.

St. Joseph's Catholic Church, 48th and Hermitage, ca. 1916. Organized in 1889, this was the first of three Polish parishes in the district. The present Romanesque style building, which has a seating capacity of 1,200, was erected in 1914. The parish maintains both a grammar school and a coeducational high school. Photo courtesy of *The Chicago Catholic* (formerly *The New World*).

Immaculate Heart of Mary Vicariate, 4515 S. Ashland Avenue, 1966. The Claretian Fathers missionary order came to Back of the Yards to serve its growing Mexican community in the 1930s. A decade later the congregation moved into permanent quarters in these connected storefronts. They were remodeled in the late 1950s to give the church its present appearance. Photo by Casey Prunchunas, CHS.

St. Martini Lutheran Church, 51st and Marshfield, 1971. An offshoot of Trinity Lutheran Church at 24th and Canal, the congregation of St. Martini was founded in 1884. Eight years later the church moved from 48th and Ada to its present site. Photo by Casey Prunchunas, CHS.

Alley behind 5040 S. Aberdeen, 1952. Alleys played an important role in the life of Chicago's working-class neighborhoods, serving as play areas for children and as short cuts for adults. The easiest entrance to many rear dwellings was through the alleys. Photo by Mildred Mead, CHS.

Southwest corner of 44th and Wood streets, 1959. Clusters of small commercial establishments like these, built ca. 1891, were common throughout Chicago working-class districts. They were first occupied by German and Irish immigrants and later by Poles and Lithuanians. Today the block is predominantly Mexican. Photo by Clarence W. Hines, CHS.

Polish Mountaineers' parade, 46th Street and Wolcott Avenue, ca. 1970. Regional loyalties established in the old country were maintained when European immigrants settled in America. The Polish Highlanders held their first North American Congress in 1930 in the parish of the Sacred Heart in Back of the Yards. Photo gift of Joseph Topor and the Polish Highlanders of North America, CHS.

Guardian Angel Day Nursery and Home for Working Women, 4600 S. McDowell Avenue, 1972. In 1912 the three Polish Catholic parishes in Back of the Yards organized Guardian Angel to provide housing for the single women who worked in Packingtown as well as day care for the children of working women. The home also offered the services of Polish-speaking male and female doctors and a dispensary. The building was located on notorious Whiskey Point, close to the University of Chicago Settlement House. Photo by Casey Prunchunas, CHS.

Northwest corner of 47th Street and Damen Avenue, 1973. Erected by the Back of the Yards Neighborhood Council, this sign reflects the strong sense of neighborhood identity shared by many Back of the Yards residents. Photo by Casey Prunchunas, CHS.

CANARYVILLE

Designations of Chicago community area boundaries are to some degree arbitrary and occasionally local residents complain that what has been described as one area really includes two or more separate neighborhoods. The area designated as New City is one such case, for it embraces at least two communities that are not only separated geographically but have had different developmental histories as well.

As indicated in the previous chapter, the Back of the Yards is located south and west of Packingtown. Canaryville is situated to the east of the Union Stock Yard, south of Pershing Road (39th Street). Its southern and eastern boundaries are 49th Street and the Pennsylvania Railroad tracks. The first family to settle in Canaryville was named Gaffrey and arrived in 1853, twelve years before the consolidation of the Union Stock Yard. Once the yards were established the Canaryville area began to attract large numbers of Irish and German workers, many of whom came from Bridgeport so that they could be within walking distance of jobs in the stockyards and Packingtown.

It was during this initial period of settlement that the area received its name, although there is no agreement as to how it

happened. Indeed, there are four separate stories which explain the origin of the name. The first is that the Irish called hogs canaries and that when one Irishman moved to the area east of the yards where hogs were then grazed, he announced that he was going to live among the canaries. A second story concerns the construction of the railroad through the area in the 1850s. Supposedly, as building proceeded, the Irish workers encountered a patch of woods inhabited by a number of wild canaries or birds that they identified as such, and so they named the area accordingly. The third story states simply that one of the early residents raised canaries. The fourth explanation is perhaps the most appealing. It was allegedly offered by a stockyard worker when the yards were being closed in 1971. He claimed that Canaryville owed its name to the fact that the wives of the workers decided to make the lives of their menfolk a little nicer and hung cages of canaries on the trees so that their husbands could hear the birds sing on their way home from work.

Once the yards and Packingtown opened, Canaryville attracted groups other than poor Irish or German workers. The meatpacking

industry required the services of clerks, cattle buyers, and intermediate management personnel. Moreover, the first generation of Packingtown owners did not want to be far from their investments and, beginning in the mid-1870s, the Swifts, Libbys, and Hutchinsons lined Emerald Avenue with their large houses.

Publications emanating from Canaryville were yet another indicator of the area's character. The *Drover's Journal*, edited by Sam Goodall, was founded in 1873 to serve not only the community but the whole meatpacking industry. The *Stock Yard Sun*, also edited by Goodall, served a similar purpose and was published until the mid-1920s. Churches, too, showed the influence of the well-to-do in the area. The Swift family put up the money to build the Union Avenue Methodist Church, which was completed in 1877 and is still known as "Swift's Church" in the neighborhood. This Protestant congregation was one of Chicago's most active in developing the social gospel reform movement during the last quarter of the nineteenth century.

Irish Catholics also established a parish in Canaryville. But St. Gabriel's, organized in 1880, was decidedly different from its working-class counterparts in Back of the Yards. To begin with, the present building of this church was designed by the famous Chicago architect, John W. Root. Second, Father Maurice Dorney, the almost legendary pastor of the parish, played an important role in setting the tone for the neighborhood and dominated much of its religious and social history until World War I. Father Dorney was a personal friend of many of the packers and often served as an intermediary between the Canaryville Irish and the slaughterhouse managers. He found jobs for his parishioners, persuaded the packers to make donations to the church and the needy in the stockyard neighborhoods, and helped to stave off labor problems in the yards.

The upper-and middle-class elements of the community did not remain beyond a single generation, however. These families then moved in two directions: south to Garfield Boulevard and across it into Englewood and east to the "Avenues" and into Kenwood. By 1900 the stately homes of the Swifts and other packing families had been converted into boarding houses and tenements to satisfy the needs of packinghouse and stockyard workers.

When the upper and middle class groups were present, the Irish dominated Canaryville numerically. "The Village," as some residents called it, grew rapidly in population in the 1870s and 1880s and, in the process, became home territory for some of Chicago's most colorful characters and most lurid activities. One such person was "Big Jim" O'Leary, the son of the Mrs. O'Leary whose spirited cow allegedly kicked over the lamp that started the Chicago fire. After the holocaust, the O'Leary family moved to Canaryville and "Big Jim" opened what was reputed to be the largest gambling house in the Windy City, just across the street from the main entrace to the Union Stock Yard, at the corner of Root and Halsted streets. The gambling and saloon business prospered, allowing the O'Leary family to move to Englewood, where they purchased a home on Garfield Boulevard. By the early 1920s, however, Canaryville had had long given up its role as a gambling center.

At this point Canaryville experienced a significant ethnic shift, as Mexicans moved into some of the more run-down sections of the neighborhood, especially those streets which immediately paralleled the Pennsylvania Railroad tracks, the eastern boundary of Canaryville. Those blocks remain heavily populated by Mexicans in the 1970s, although this group is now spread more evenly throughout the neighborhood. The Mexican component of Canaryville is still numerically smaller than the Spanish-speaking group located in the Back of the Yards. The Puerto Rican population remains small.

Blacks also have come to Canaryville during the last few years. While the expansion of the black belt in the 1950s brought a complete racial transition in Fuller Park, the neighborhood just east of Canaryville, the latter area remained Irish and Mexican. During the next decade, the black belt expanded to the area just south of Canaryville, and since 1970 this stretch, especially south of 49th, has become predominantly black. White Southerners who have recently migrated to the city can also be found in the Canaryville neighborhood.

Throughout Canaryville's history, Halsted, which separates the neighborhood from the stockyards, has been the main business street, with Halsted and Exchange the principal intersection around which businesses clustered. Since Exchange was the entrance street into the yards, establishments preferred to be as close as possible to the intersection. The southwest corner of Exchange and Halsted was, for more than a century, the site of a hostelry that catered to those who came to the yards or Packingtown. Known as the Hough House at the time of its construction in 1865, this hotel was later renamed the Transit House. After the building burned in 1911 it was rebuilt and named the Stock Yard Inn. It burned again in 1934 and was rebuilt and reopened in 1935. The construction of the new International Amphitheatre in 1934 at 42nd and Halsted was good for the hotel's business. The Stock Yard Inn continued to thrive through the early 1960s, when the Amphitheatre became a convention center, then fell on hard times. Before it was finally torn down in 1977, the Inn had housed such diverse celebrities as Dwight Eisenhower and Elvis Presley.

The other type of business that flourished along Halsted across from the yards was the saloon. Such establishments did not serve the neighborhood but catered to the numerous visitors who came to the stockyards or to the entertainment and sporting events held at the Dexter Park Amphitheatre or the Dexter Park Race Track located at 47th and Halsted. Before Prohibition, forty-two saloons lined Halsted between Root and 42nd. When Prohibition ended and the International Amphitheatre opened, the taverns returned. Some remain open to the present day. One, the Horn Palace, which gained a national reputation when it served as FBI headquarters during the Democratic National Convention of 1968, had been a hangout for cowboys and truckers in the days when the stockyards and the exhibition hall were in full operation.

On the southwest corner of 45th and

Halsted, formerly stockyard property, there is a Union 76 Truck Stop of the kind that can be found along interstate highways. It is an ironic reminder of the technological change which spelled the doom of the Union Stock Yard. For the conversion from railroad transportation to trucking was one important factor in bringing about the exodus of meatpacking plants from Chicago. By 1960 a majority of livestock sold at the yards arrived by truck, and at its closing in 1971, this figure had increased to over 95 percent. Trucking allowed the packers to replace their large obsolete plants with numerous smaller, more efficient ones closer to sources of livestock and out of immediate reach of urban air and water pollution laws. But the Union 76 Truck Stop is also indicative of another factor in Chicago's changing economic life. The truck stop site was previously part of the Armour and Company Car Shops which provided the city with both jobs and tax revenue. Today the area is mainly a parking lot, providing few jobs and little tax income.

When the stockyards fell on hard times in the early 1960s, an attempt was made to bring new life to Canaryville by allowing the construction of a Community Discount Center at the northwest corner of 47th and Halsted. Originally the location of the Dexter Park Race Track, it was also the site on which the first major league baseball game—between the Chicago White Stockings (now the Chicago Cubs) and the Cincinnati Red Legs—was played in 1877. After the race track was closed, the corner became a coal yard which served the South Side until the Discount Center was constructed on this site. When the retail installation was opened there were predictions that it would bring new prosperity to the local community. Actually it brought as many

St. Gabriel's Catholic Church, 4552 S. Wallace Avenue. Designed by Chicago architect John Root, this reddish-brown brick church was constructed in 1887. Root claimed that the 160-foot tower, topped by a stone cross, was the only church spire in the city fashioned entirely of masonry. Poetess Harriet Monroe described the church as being "as personal as the clasp of [the architect's] hand." Photo courtesy of the Newberry Library.

problems as it did income. The black districts to the east and south of Canaryville have very few shopping areas, especially since the decline of the 63rd and Halsted district. The Community Discount Center was sufficiently large to attract customers from east and west as well as north and south. Thus it became a place where the races met, and not always on pleasant terms. Canaryville and Back of the Yards residents have therefore come to view this shopping center as contributing to the racial instability of their neighborhoods.

This perception might be less important were it not for the fact that 47th Street east of Halsted to the Penn Central tracks was never a well-built area and has been clearly deteriorating over the past couple of decades. The old United Charities Building, located at 47th and Emerald, which now houses Thresholds South, reflects the street's variegated character along these blocks. The building was erected in 1914 as "a new kind of social service center for welfare agencies," an institutional attempt to deal with the social and medical problems of the stockyard district. Its clients now are mostly black and Mexican.

Many Irish families have, however, remained in the Canaryville neighborhood, where they continue to maintain their Irish-American traditions, especially those associated with the parish life of St. Gabriel's. The Irish pattern of mobility in the city, meanwhile, is exemplified in the fortunes of the Thomas McInerney's Sons Funeral Parlor. This establishment got its start in Canaryville, and, while the owners have opened another branch in the far southwest side of the city, they have also maintained the original location. The working-class Irish of Canaryville seem to have remained closer to their ethnic heritage than most of their middle-class cousins in the neighborhoods located southwest of the 1850s settlement. Indeed, Canaryville—often referred to as Shanty Town by the more affluent of the Chicago Irish—remains the closest thing to a solidly Irish working-class neighborhood to be found in the city.

"Big Jim" O'Leary's Saloon, 4183–85 S. Halsted Street, 1906. The saloon bearing the name of "Chicago's real and only gambler king" was exclusively a drinking establishment. O'Leary's gambling parlor was at 4187 S. Halsted, just south of the saloon, and contained a maze of secret rooms where "Big Jim" made his reputation. Then and now that building also housed a hardware and paint store. *Chicago Daily News* photo, gift of Field Enterprises, CHS.

Thomas Gahan Public Bath House, 4226–28 S. Wallace Street, 1958. Public baths were important in the lives of poor and working-class city dwellers who had no bathrooms in their crowded tenements. Named for a politician who grew wealthy in sewer, drainage, canal, and gas company contracting, this bath was opened in 1907 at a cost of $19,500. Photo by John McCarthy, CHS.

Family Services Bureau, 734 W. 47th Street, 1974. Built in 1914 with funds provided by the United Charities, this structure originally housed United Charities offices, a maternity dispensary of Chicago Lying-In Hospital, a dispensary of the Municipal Tuberculosis Sanitarium, the Stockyards Dental Dispensary, and a sub-station of the Juvenile Protective Association. Today it is used by Thresholds South, a mental health rehabilitation agency. Photo by Casey Prunchunas, CHS.

Tilden High School, 4747 S. Union Avenue, 1977. Formerly named Lake High School, Tilden became part of the Chicago school system following the annexation of the Town of Lake in 1889. The original building, erected in 1887, was replaced in 1905. Ten years later the name was changed to Tilden Technical High School. The school became a regular high school again in 1963, when Lindbloom High School took over technical instruction for the district. Photo by Glen E. Holt, CHS.

536–544 W. 47th Street, 1974. Three of these buildings were erected before 1891 at what was then the very edge of settlement in Canaryville; to the south lay open prairie. After World War I, the use of asbestos and asphalt siding became a popular way to renew old wooden buildings and also served as an early form of insulation. Photo by Casey Prunchunas, CHS.

Union Avenue United Methodist Church, 4356 S. Union Avenue, 1953. This congregation was founded in 1877 at the home of meatpacking magnate Gustavus F. Swift. For a time, the well-known "Social Gospel" minister, the Reverend Harry S. Ward, was the pastor of this church. Photo by Arthur M. Weiland, CHS.

Wooden cottage, 4645 S. Union Avenue, 1977. This cottage was built in the 1880s at the rear of the lot, but a front structure was never erected. Until 1885, most of the housing in this area consisted of cottages; there-after, multi-family units became common. Photo by Glen E. Holt, CHS.

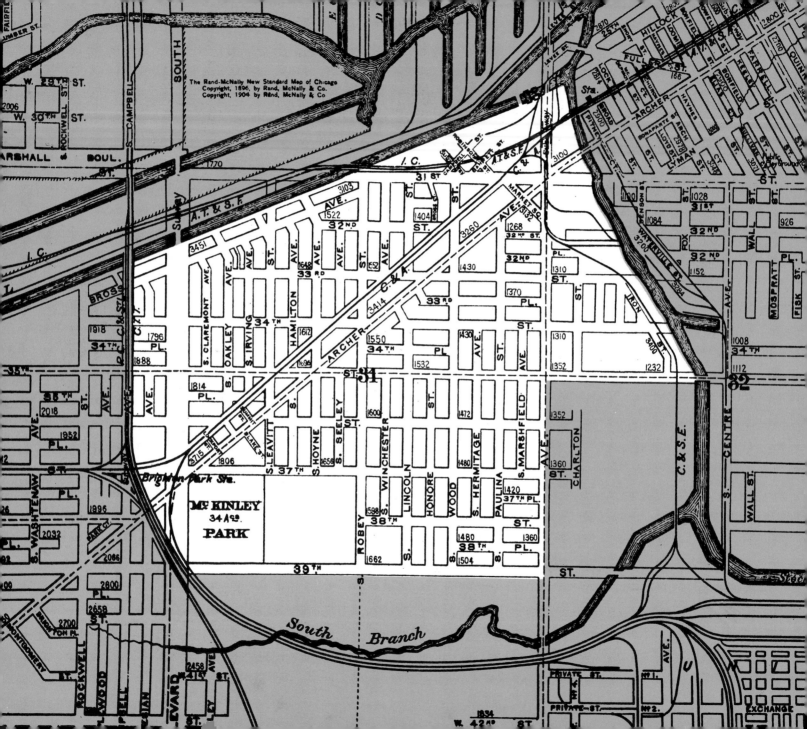

MᶜKINLEY PARK

McKinley Park is a neighborhood blessed with three "natural" boundaries which make for considerable stability: the South Fork of the South Branch of the Chicago River to the east, the Stevenson Expressway and the Illinois and Michigan Canal to the north, and the tracks of the Penn Central Railroad to the west. The southern boundary is 39th Street. Cutting diagonally through the neighborhood is Archer Avenue, which is paralleled on its northern side by the Gulf, Mobile and Ohio Railroad.

Among Chicago neighborhoods, the McKinley Park area has one of the longest histories. When construction began on the Illinois and Michigan Canal in 1836, a few Irish families took out squatters' rights on small tracts in what later became the community area. The land on which these cottages were built was generally low and marshy. In the early 1840s some farmers purchased land in the area, drained it, and chased off the Irish. Among the first of these newcomers was the Beers family. In 1847 the Beers put down their roots in a plot of land just west of Ashland, choosing the area because it reminded them of the timberland of their native New England. The Beers farm was subdivided into urban lots in 1882.

Urban settlement attempts in McKinley Park began in the 1830s. The first "town" to be subdivided was Canalport, which straddled the South Branch of the Chicago River. The western half of this paper town was in the future neighborhood of McKinley Park. Canalport never achieved the residential status that its developers had anticipated, because Bridgeport was better sited and had more jobs close by.

While Canalport, to the east of McKinley Park, was unsuccessful, the town of Brighton, located at its southwest corner, developed quickly. Brighton was platted in 1840 and incorporated eleven years later. The two principal attractions in Brighton were its magnificent race course, which appealed to Chicago's early race horse owners and gamblers, and the Brighton Stock Yards, which lay north of Archer Avenue.

The opening of the Illinois and Michigan Canal in 1848 stimulated further subdivision in the McKinley Park area, as did the coming of the Chicago and Alton Railroad in 1857. Industry began to locate heavily in the area during the Civil War decade and by 1870 the working-class character of McKinley Park was set.

One of the important early industries in McKinley Park was a steel mill which opened in 1863. This factory, which later became part of Illinois Steel, was located at Archer and Ashland. Many of its employees settled in a small triangle bordered by Ashland, Archer, and 35th. This unincorporated settlement was called Mt. Pleasant. Although the steel mill was closed when Illinois Steel built a new mill in South Chicago in 1896, the tiny residential area maintained its traditional designation for several decades longer.

The name Mt. Pleasant seems ironic not only because of the adjacent steel mill but also because of the character of the surrounding landscape. In the 1860s most areas of McKinley Park were still swampy and undrained. Each spring when the rains fell, the prairie sloughs filled with water and became breeding grounds for mosquitos. To avoid the risk of flood some houses had to be built on stilts. Because of the perennial flooding and standing water, the section of Archer Avenue in what is now the community area acquired the appellation of Ducktown. Some Ducktown landowners, in an attempt to raise their land out of the water, rendered the area even less salubrious by allowing scavenger companies to dump their ashes in the low-lying spots. The scavengers immediately took advantage of the situation and dumped not only ashes but every kind of junk and garbage as well. They continued this practice even after the area of McKinley Park was incorporated into the city of Chicago in 1863. Until sewers and formal drainage lines were established, piled up garbage and ashes only made the environment worse, for the filling cut natural drainage lines, and the pools of dirty water stood longer than they had before the filling began.

After the fire of 1871, industries were built along three sides of McKinley Park. Within five years, eleven new factories opened in the community, most of them manufacturing iron and steel products. During the same period, twenty-seven brickyards operated within the area. The meat plants of Packingtown just south of the neighborhood were also opened in the 1870s. The packing plants had a particularly negative impact on the environment of the eastern half of the neighborhood, for they dumped their waste material from the slaughtering process into the South Branch of the Chicago River.

Until 1921 the South Side Chicago River system was much larger than it is at present. Beginning in that year, the city closed the old Stock Yard Slip and proceeded to cover up the West Fork which flowed through the packinghouse district adjacent to the stockyards. Until it was filled, the West Fork had a unique character for a waterway. Neighborhood residents claimed that birds could walk across the stream because of the thick crust of fat and other waste material from the packinghouses. Another neighborhood story tells of small children who attempted to walk across the river, broke through the crust, and were never seen again. During the race riot of 1919 reports were circulated

that the West Branch was filled with the bodies of rioters. But the most interesting piece of folklore about "Bubbly Creek," as the West Fork was called, concerns Gustavus Swift, the founder of Swift and Company. It is said that while walking along the edge of the creek where his plant was located, Swift noticed the large amount of fat that was flowing from his packinghouse into the river. He immediately ordered an end to this wasteful process and then organized a crew of workers who were sent out on Bubbly Creek in small boats to skim the surface for fat and return it to the Swift plant for rendering.

Industrial development continued in McKinley Park throughout the remainder of the nineteenth century, and numerous foreignborn groups moved to the neighborhood to take advantage of its employment opportunities. Irish, Germans, English, Welsh, Swedes, and native-born Americans arrived in the 1870s, with more Germans, Irish, and Swedes coming in the course of the next decade. While the Irish were the predominant ethnic group, the area remained the most American of all the settlements in the stockyard districts. Even after 1900, when the Poles and other East Europeans began to arrive in large numbers and a gypsy camp grew up at 45th and Western, English continued to be the street language of the community.

Transit lines reached the community in the late 1880s and 1890s. They first ran on Archer Avenue, the second on 35th. Even before these transit lines were installed, the intersection of the two streets formed the commercial center of McKinley Park. The existence of the 47th and Ashland commercial district, however, prevented this shopping center from becoming fully articulated. Instead, the two streets became commercial

strips that cut through the neighborhood, and the "store" that predominated was the saloon.

More recently, the community has been bisected by another street development which serves to divide it even more than either Archer or 35th. The intent of the Damen Avenue Overpass, which connected 37th and 47th streets in 1962, was to provide a north-south feeder into the still unbuilt Stevenson Expressway. The overpass was erected on piers over the yards of the Chicago Junction Railroad, which services the Central Manufacturing District and the old Union Stock Yard area. The completion of the overpass marked an end to years of neglect for Damen Avenue.

Originally known as Long John (in honor of Chicago's colorful mayor, John Wentworth, who had opened the Brighton Park Race Track in 1855) the street was renamed Robey in 1863, after James Robey, a realestate developer who lived on the corner of Robey and Washington on the city's West Side. On June 15, 1927, the City Council changed the name of the street once more, this time to Damen Avenue, in honor of Father Arnold Damen, who had organized the Holy Family Parish on the West Side, and, in 1862, established the Jesuit institution which would become Loyola University of Chicago. These changes in name, however, were not matched by any improvement in the condition of this thoroughfare, which, until the construction of the Damen overpass in 1961, was blocked by the Chicago Junction yards.

The city did make significant improvements in McKinley Park in the 1880s at the time that the Illinois and Sanitary Ship Canal was being dug parallel with the outmoded Illinois and Michigan Canal. Public sewers were installed and packed rock was put

McKinley Monument in McKinley Park, ca. 1909. This statue of the assassinated president (designed by Charles J. Mulligan and recast from the bronze of a much disliked statue of Columbus which once stood in Grant Park), was dedicated in 1905. Sculptor Lorado Taft hailed it as "a dignified and serious piece of sculpture." Photo by George R. Lawrence, CHS.

down in the area's major streets. The city also built some new schools, notably the Brighton School (later renamed Longfellow Elementary), in the area. These improvements were made at a critical time for the neighborhood, when the brickyards which had employed many of the residents had closed down. In 1896 the Illinois Steel Company closed its plant, which had employed as many as 1,500 workers at its peak. Thereafter, McKinley Park workers found themselves increasingly dependent upon Packingtown for employment.

From this low point came the community's most important landmark and its name. In the late 1890s, three prominent South Siders, motivated by that combination of altruism and desire for profits which has inspired so many urban developments, began pressing for the construction of a large park on the old Brighton Park Race Track property. Contractor Dan Crilly, legislator Dave Shanahan, and meatpacker Philip D. Armour, were instrumental in this undertaking, which was already under way when President William McKinley was assassinated. The new park and, eventually, the entire neighborhood, were named after the late president.

The park encouraged new residential construction. Before 1900, McKinley Park houses were mostly wooden balloon-frame structures, cheaply built and quickly erected. After the turn of the century, single-family and two-flat brick structures catering to working-class families continued to predominate but they were of better quality than any residential buildings erected previously in the neighborhood. Coinciding with the dedication of McKinley Park, the area experienced two different—but by no means unrelated—industrial developments. In 1902 a New Jersey corporation began ac-

quiring the land on both sides of the South Branch of the Chicago River. By 1908 this group had a parcel of 260 acres, and during the next seven years most of it was filled by the buildings of the Central Manufacturing District. The second industrial development was the installation of the Crane Company's largest manufacturing plant in Chicago. The Crane Company is best known for its bathroom fixtures, but its initial development in McKinley Park included facilities for the manufacture of steam and water piping for large industrial plants like those in neighboring Packingtown. On the one hand, these developments brought new jobs to the community; on the other hand, the need for space for industrial development led to the razing of many of the old wooden cottages which had originally housed the canal workers and later the employees of the early steel mills and brickyards.

McKinley Park was residentially mature before World War I broke out. Its 1920 population count of 22,016 remained stable for a decade, increasing to only 22,032 by 1930. Of that total, 77.3 percent were either foreign born or the sons and daughters of foreign born. Nearly half of this group was Polish, followed by the Germans, with the Irish placing a far-behind third. That ethnic character has continued to the present. In 1970, 33.1 percent of all foreign-born in McKinley Park were from Poland, while among children of foreign-born, those of Polish stock constituted 44.1 percent. The respective figures for the Germans were 13.6 percent and 13.5 percent.

The composition of the population was the only stable feature in McKinley Park between 1930 and 1970. Other changes were gradual, however. From a population peak of 22,032 in 1930, the total number of inhabitants in the area dropped by 28.7 per-

cent to 15,701 in 1970. This loss was paralleled by a similar drop in jobs available in nearby plants. The Central Manufacturing District is employing far fewer persons than it was two decades ago, the giant Crane Company plant is largely used for warehousing, and Packingtown has disappeared.

Moreover, the people of McKinley Park are older than they were forty years ago. In 1930 only 3.4 percent were aged 65 and over, while in 1960 that figure had risen to 9.5 percent, where it remained through the next decade. Just as the population of McKinley Park is growing older, so too is the housing. Of the total habitable units in the community in 1970, 91.4 percent were built before 1940. Of these 27.6 percent were detached single-family structures, 39.5 percent were two flats, and 22.4 percent were in three-or four-unit buildings. The age of the housing does not, however, denote poverty, for 52.2 percent of the families earn between $10,000 and $25,000 per year. The median income for the whole neighborhood is $10,781. There are two reasons why family incomes are relatively high. First, among the males in the work force, 21 percent are craftsmen or foremen. An additional 37.5 percent are in clerical, operative, and transport worker categories. Second, a large number of women also work, 49.2 percent of them being employed in clerical positions and an additional 18.5 percent in factories, thus providing additional income.

McKinley Park, then, maintains its position as a white working-class ethnic neighborhood. The only recent newcomers are Spanish-Americans. Between 1960 and 1970, 970 Spanish-Americans moved to McKinley Park, accounting for 6.2 percent of the total neighborhood population in the latter year. The reasons why McKinley Park has maintained its working-class character can be found not only in employment patterns but also in the neighborhood's boundaries. As in all cities, the population of Chicago is involved in ceaseless changes of location, sometimes rapid, sometimes slow. McKinley Park, with "natural boundaries" along three sides, and partially protected on its southern edge by installations of the Central Manufacturing District, can be viewed as an "eddy" in the continuing current. The area is not stagnant or unchanging, however. The 1960 census recorded that 39 percent of all families had moved from a different household in the previous five years. The 1970 figure was an even higher 42.9. However, the part of the housing stock associated with the highest degree of mobility, rental units, is declining, while home ownership has been increasing. In 1940, 59.3 percent of all dwelling units were renter-occupied while 38.7 percent were owner-occupied. The comparable figures for 1970 were 51.7 percent and 45.9 percent.

The critical element in the future of McKinley Park appears to be its housing stock. If replacement of worn-out houses or remodeling occurs at an accelerated pace, there are grounds for an optimistic view of this neighborhood's future. The people who live there already appear to have adjusted to the declining job rate in the immediate area by the simple process of using public transit and their automobiles to get back and forth to work in other areas. If the Central Manufacturing District takes on new life or if new manufacturing is brought to Packingtown, then the future of McKinley Park could be very bright.

St. Philippus United Church of Christ, 2040 W. 36th Street, 1971. A group of Germans, most of whom had moved to McKinley Park from neighborhoods to the northeast, founded this church in 1902. Photo by Casey Prunchunas, CHS.

Longfellow School, 1901 W. 35th Street, 1971. This building, which is still in use, was erected in 1880; an addition was built in 1886. Known originally as the Lincoln Street and Douglas Avenue School, it was renamed the Brighton School in 1880 and finally became the

Longfellow School in 1904. Its architecture was common to schools built in Chicago's working-class districts during the last quarter of the nineteenth century. Photo by Sigmund J. Osty, CHS.

Bubbly Creek, 1959. The south fork of the
South Branch of the Chicago River, Bubbly
Creek forms the eastern boundary of
McKinley Park. Notorious as an open sewer for
the packinghouses which once lined its
banks, the waterway helped to give the stockyard area its special ambience. The
river today is much smaller than it once was,
but its surface still erupts with bubbles
from the pollutants decomposing on the creek's
bottom. Photo by John McCarthy, CHS.

1936–1944 W. 35th Street, 1970. All these houses
were erected before 1890 on land originally
held by the trustees of the Illinois and Michigan
Canal. The four brick structures either pre-
dated or simply disregarded the raising of the
street grade along 35th Street, a fact reflected
in their ramp stairs and second floor entrances.
Photo by Sigmund J. Osty, CHS.

Rowhouses, 3500 block of S. Honore, 1950. This notorious tenement was erected before 1886 to house workers employed in the expanding industries of the district. The strip was known locally as "Outhouse Alley" because the units had no indoor plumbing and outdoor privies stood in a neat line behind the houses. Such rowhouses were unusual in McKinley Park and other stockyard neighborhoods. Photo by Mildred Mead, CHS.

Corner saloon, 1635 W. 35th Street, 1972. This building, the first on the lot, was constructed between 1887 and 1891. The introduction of public transportation to McKinley Park during this period increased the comings and goings in the area and brought many customers to such strategically located corner saloons. Photo by Casey Prunchunas, CHS.

BRIGHTON PARK

Brighton Park at first glance seems larger than it really is. Its boundaries—the Stevenson Expressway and the Illinois Michigan Canal on the north, the Chicago River and Indiana Railroad tracks on the south, the Santa Fe Railroad on the west, and the Penn Central on the east—encompass a community area of between six and seven square miles. However, because railroad lines and yards cut into and through the community, the total living and work space in the neighborhood is only about two-thirds of that area.

This neighborhood, which owes its initial existence to the building of Archer Avenue and the Blue Island Plank Road (Western Avenue), is older than its neighboring communities of McKinley Park and Back of the Yards, even though the latter are closer to the center of the city. The original unincorporated subdivision of Brighton was dedicated as early as 1840. At that time its boundaries were 35th on the north, Western on the east, Wright (now the tracks of the Chicago and Alton Railroad) on the south; and Blanchard Avenue (now Rockwell) on the west. Brighton Park was incorporated as a village in 1851 by the land development company which built the Blue Island Plank Road. By the mid-1850s the village hosted two of Chicago's most important industries: gambling and livestock trading. Southeast of the village, in what is now McKinley Park, was "Long John" Wentworth's Brighton Park Race Track, while the Brighton Stock Yards and Drovers' Hotel were located at the corner of Archer and Western. With some basis in fact, these latter facilities were alleged to be the finest in the West for the marketing of livestock.

Brighton Park's significance as a livestock center faded as new railroad lines entering Chicago presented better marketing options. By 1859 three other yards were offering serious competition as railroads displaced the cattle drives which had formerly come north on Western or northeast on Archer Avenue. In an attempt to revive the Brighton Yards, its owners in 1861 persuaded the United States Agricultural Society to hold a state fair at the Brighton livestock market. The Chicago and St. Louis Railroad agreed to provide special train service directly to the fair for both livestock and passengers. But inclement weather turned the Brighton state fair into a disaster and the Brighton exchange owners never recovered from the venture. The opening of the Union Stock Yard in 1865 about one and one-half miles east of Brighton Park killed all remaining business and the neighborhood quickly fell under the growing shadow of the districts to the east.

The Brighton Park Race Track remained a popular meeting place both for racing and for annual celebrations like the Fourth of July for some years longer. But just as the success of the Union Stock Yard killed the Brighton Livestock Exchange so the success of the Dexter Park Race Track (owned and operated by the Union Stock Yard and Transit Company) led to the closing of the Brighton Race Track. In 1870 "Long John" Wentworth, making the best of a bad situation, leased the race track land to truck farmers, who turned it into a cabbage patch to provide raw material for the manufacture of sauerkraut. In 1901 this land was absorbed into Chicago's South Parks system as McKinley Park.

The passing of the livestock industry did not signal an end to the economic development of this area. When the Civil War ended, Chicago needed stone as a building material and Brighton Park became the center of a construction-oriented explosives industry. In 1866 Matthew Laflin established the first powder mill in Brighton. He chose the district in order to be close to the limestone and other quarries which were located southwest of the city. After Laflin's arrival the explosives industry grew rapidly and haphazardly. On August 29, 1886, Brighton Park was rocked by a tremendous explosion at the Laflin and Rand Company Powder Mill. The next day a mass meeting of nearby residents condemned the powder houses as unsafe and called for their removal. Eventually the industry moved to suburban Blue Island, a few miles south of Brighton Park.

Other industries came to Brighton as part of the post-Civil War industrialization that swept through Chicago. The Brighton Cotton Mill was established in 1871–72 and, in the following year, the Brighton Silver Smelting and Refining Company. Brickyards also moved into the district, one of the largest being at the intersection of Kedzie Avenue and the Illinois and Michigan Canal. Another was the yard of the O.L. Mann Brick Company at Archer and California, now the site of Kelly Park. Railroads, which had first run through the district in the 1850s, continued to expand in the area. In the early 1870s the Chicago and Alton Railroad set up its roundhouse and repair shops in the neighborhood. The most important railroad development for the future, however, occurred in 1887, when the Santa Fe Railroad established its Corwith freight yards at 35th and Central Park Avenue. These yards are still among the largest switching facilities in the nation.

The continued industrialization of the district brought new residents. The earliest settlers of Brighton Park had been native Americans, Germans, and Irish. In the 1870s the latter two groups were in the majority. The new arrivals for the most part settled along Western Avenue near the former stockyards and race track. Farms still occupied a portion of the neighborhood, especially that part south of 39th Street (Pershing Road), west of California. A small settlement also developed between Pershing Road and 43rd Street, just west of Western Avenue, in a part of Brighton Park that was within the Town of Lake. The greater part of the neighborhood, however, consisted of low marshy land that had to be drained before settlement could occur. It would take annexation to Chicago in 1889 to spark land speculation in all of Brighton Park, especially in the southern half, and drainage and the building of new residences soon followed.

In 1878, Irish Catholics who had moved to Brighton Park petitioned for a local parish because they were now too far from St. Bridget's, of which many had formerly been communicants. The request was granted and full parish status was conferred that same year. The first church home was a cottage on California, just south of 38th. A new, larger church building and school were erected at 39th and Washtenaw in 1884. German Lutherans attended St. Andrew's Church, which had been formed in McKinley Park in 1888 at 36th and Wood. In 1902 the Peace Lutheran Church congregation was organized and, the following year, a new church and school were dedicated at 43rd and Mozart. The present building and school, located at the southwest corner of California and 43rd, dates from 1911.

The expansion of the railroad which criss-crossed the prairie of Brighton Park during the 1880s and 1890s, had two important effects on the development of the area. First, it encouraged future industrial growth, especially the creation of the Central Manufacturing District's Crawford Avenue project. Second, it made Brighton Park into a commuter suburb and, consequently, increased the demand for housing. The area's accessibility was further increased by the improvement of local transportation. In 1898 the Western Avenue horsecar line was put into operation, supplementing the line which ran down Archer to what is now Pulaski Road. A line on 47th Street also reached Kedzie Avenue, tying Brighton Park to the stockyards district. These latter developments enabled some better-paid packinghouse workers to move out of the neighborhood immediately adjoining the yards to the Brighton Park neighborhood.

Increased access attracted new groups to the neighborhood. The 1890s saw the construction of numerous balloon-frame cottages and some double-deckers in the area north of Pershing Road. This area attracted new emigrants from the city, with two groups in particular in evidence, one French, the other Jewish. Like other Catholic groups, the French signalled their arrival by founding a parish in 1889, the parish of St. Joseph and St. Ann. A group of Eastern European Jews settled in the northwestern corner of the neighborhood. But their stay there was brief, for they soon moved to North Lawndale, leaving behind only a small enclave of merchants. Germans and Irish remained the principal nationality groups in residence: they either had the money and the time for a short commute into the yards, or they had taken better jobs in the new industrial areas which were being built up along the railroad line that ringed the neighborhood. However, Brighton Park still fell short of offering the comforts of a suburban retreat. Its streets remained unpaved and the level of its city services was low.

Between 1900 and 1925, Brighton Park experienced its most rapid phase of deve-

Detail of an engraving of a hog drive headed for Chicago, 1868. Even after the advent of the railroad, large herds of hogs and other livestock were transported to Chicago on the hoof. Before the establishment of the Union Stock Yard, such drives often ended at the Brighton Stock Yard. From *Harper's Weekly,* October 31, 1868, CHS.

DRIVING HOGS TO THE CHICAGO MARKET.—[See Page 702.]

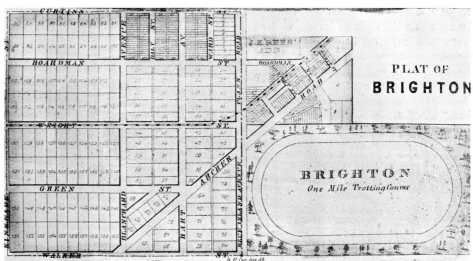

Plat of Brighton, 1861. In the first Brighton settlement developers made the lots narrow so that as many as possible could have a frontage along Archer Road. Those near the railroad were larger and were used as sites for warehouses or manufacturing establishments. From *Map of Cook County, Illinois,* 1861, CHS.

lopment and reached residential maturity. The first factor in this quickening of pace was expanding industrialization. The opening of the Central Manufacturing District north of the Union Stock Yard proved a prelude to Brighton Park's own development. In 1915 the Crane Company opened its giant Corwith plant on Kedzie Avenue near Pershing in the northwest quadrant of Brighton Park. At the same time, the Kenwood Manufacturing District was being established along the southern edge of the neighborhood.

These new employment opportunities created the need for new residences and the section of Brighton Park south of Pershing Road was now built up with small brick single-family dwellings or brick two-flats. The erection of this latter type of housing is especially significant, for a two-flat provided its owner with a home for his family as well as rental income from the second flat. By combining the rental income with his own payment he could handle a larger mortgage than would otherwise be possible. As this period of heavy construction was taking place, the city began to install physical services throughout the neighborhood. By now the automobile had joined mass transit as a means of commuting to work, and by 1925 Brighton Park was residentially mature.

During the early phase of this massive development, two new ethnic groups, Poles and Lithuanians, began to move into Brighton Park. Many of these newcomers either bought the new two-flat buildings or rented one of the units. By 1909 sufficient Poles had moved to the neighborhood to warrant the establishment of the Polish parish of Five Holy Martyrs. The Lithuanians organized the parish of the Immaculate Conception in 1914. The following year the Lithuanian Sisters of St. Casimir opened a

TOWN OF BRIGHTON.

This new town, to be found laid down on this map, at the junction of Blue Island Avenue and the Archer Road, is less than one mile from the City limits. The land is high, and during the wet season is kept well drained and is never under water. The soil is among the richest in the county, and having now a planked avenue and bridges across the canal and west branch of the river, afford an easy and short access to the heart of the city, offering great inducements for the cultivation of Gardens to supply our markets. It is designed, early in the Spring, to erect a suitable Hotel, with convenient stables, yards, scales and every appendage for an extensive Live Stock Market, and to have a line of OMNIBUSSES running to it.

It is known, that at Chicago **THERE ARE MORE CATTLE SLAUGHTERED** and packed than at any other city in the United States, and for *this trade alone* there is a "Brighton" at Boston and other cities in the East, and at Cincinnati in the West, and it is now determined to add this to the number—to excel them all. BRIGHTON will thus from its location and many advantages become an important centre for a large suburban settlement, and offers peculiar advantages for investments, as the whole of it is now offered in Lots, giving all disposed a chance to buy.

The terms are very easy, being one-tenth cash, and one-tenth every three months thereafter.

☞ For number and size of Lots, see annexed Catalogue.

Advertisement for the town of Brighton, 1853–54. This early real estate broadside indicates that the settlement did not take its name from the race track, as most sources state, but from the traditional designation for livestock markets in Britain and the Eastern United States. From *Map of Chicago and its Southern & Western Suburbs*, 1853, CHS.

parish school. The compact settlements of the older Irish and German inhabitants of Brighton Park gave way as more Poles, Lithuanians, and Italians flooded the area. In 1924 another Polish parish, St. Pancratius, was organized for the newcomers.

Since this great immigration of the 1910s and 1920s, the Poles have dominated Brighton Park. In 1930 foreign-born Poles and their children made up 37 percent of all residents, who in that census reached their peak number of 46,552. In 1970 those who were Polish born made up 34.8 percent of the total population of 35,614, while the Poles who were sons or daughters of foreign-born parents constituted 45 percent. Today, Brighton Park is the most heavily Polish neighborhood in the city, surpassing even the large Polish settlements previously located in West Town and Humboldt Park on the near Northwest Side.

While the statistics on nativity lead to a fairly clear-cut conclusion, housing data for the neighborhood shows another long-run trend. As the population decreased from 45,552 in 1940 to 35,614 in 1970, the number of housing units increased from 11,566 to 12,958. During the past forty-year period, ownership has risen from 39.8 percent of all units to 47.6 percent. Thus, over the last four decades, home ownership has increased as population has decreased. The explanation is to be found in the age of the population. The people of the neighborhood quite simply have grown older. In 1930 only 14.4 percent of Brighton Park residents were 45 years old or older. By 1960 that figure had risen to 32.2 percent.

Over the years the population has maintained its working-class character. In 1970, 52.7 percent of Brighton Park families had annual incomes between $10,000 and $25,000. Nearly 86 percent of all employed adults worked in private industry. And to hold those jobs, slightly more than 45 percent of all these workers commuted. This means that Brighton Park functions like a typical post-World War II residential suburb, its residents being heavily dependent on the auto. Those who pay rent pay a mean of $80 per month compared to $115 for the city as a whole, while the mean value of owner units is $17,116 compared to $22,752 for the city. It is an ironic fact that rents in Brighton Park are lower than those in neighborhoods to the southeast of the stockyards, such as Washington Park or Woodlawn, even though the housing stock in Brighton Park is in much better condition.

Brighton Park continues to be a community of upwardly-mobile ethnic groups, with the older Polish and Lithuanian residents having succeeded the Germans, Irish, and native white Americans who dominated in former years. The newer groups remain dominant although during the last decade Spanish-speaking groups have begun to move into this area. The neighborhood remains attractive because of its relatively low rents, reasonable mortgages, and good housing conditions as well as its fine parochial and public schools. There is a mounting fear of racial change manifested by several demonstrations over the past few years at Kelly High School, but basically the neighborhood seems stable and vital.

4307 S. Kedzie Avenue, 1967. Such single-family workers' cottages are among the oldest structures in Brighton Park; many were constructed in the 1890s. Photo by Ann Maksymiec, CHS.

Power Ford Agency, 4400 S. Archer Avenue, 1971. This terra cotta structure was built for the Archer Buick Company in 1928. In 1950 the building was taken over by the Hannah Motor Truck Sales; its present tenant, Power Ford, moved in ten years later. Photo by Joe Domin, CHS.

Slowik Clothing Store, 4328 S. Archer Avenue, 1965. Polish and Lithuanian names are common among business establishments in Brighton Park. Photo by Ann Maksymiec, CHS.

Union hall, United Steelworkers of America, 4145 S. Kedzie Avenue, 1968. Local 2047 served the workers of the Crane Manufacturing Company, which was located across the street from the hall. Photo by Ann Maksymiec, CHS.

Brick two-flat, 4219 S. Kedzie Avenue, 1965. Dwellings like these began to be built in Brighton Park in the 1910s. More spacious two-flats were also erected before World War I, although most were constructed in the 1920s. Photo by Ann Maksymiec, CHS.

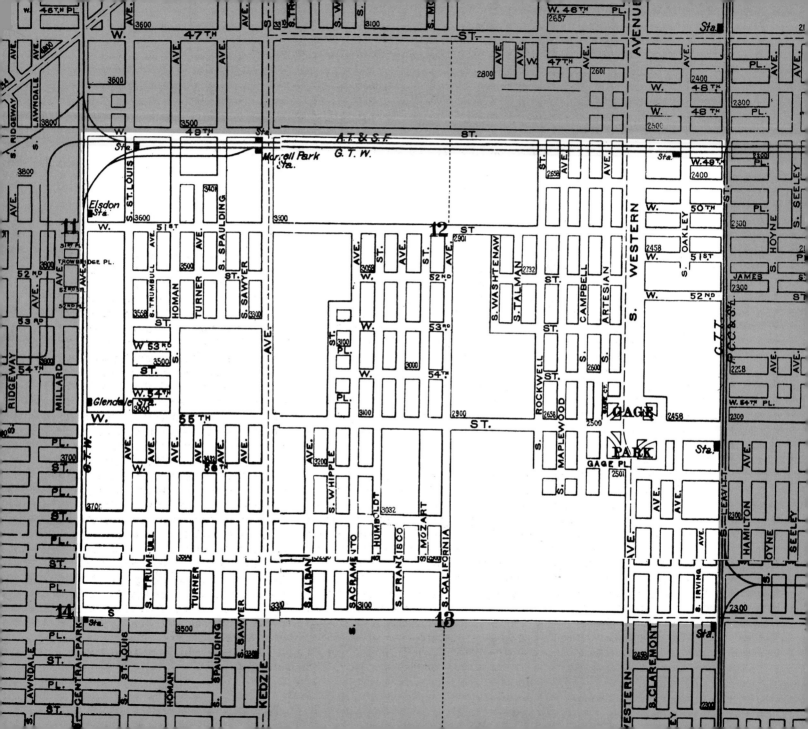

GAGE PARK

The Gage Park neighborhood is located southwest of Back of the Yards and south of Brighton Park. Bounded by railroads on the east, west, and north, it has 59th Street as its southern edge. The first settlers, many of whom were German, came to this area in the 1840s and the 1850s. They established small 5- to 10-acre truck farms in the southeast quadrant of the present neighborhood, in the area bounded by 49th and 55th, Western and California. One of the early owners of this acreage was Henry Gage, after whom Gage Park and the surrounding neighborhood were named.

When the Illinois Legislature created the South Park Commission in 1869, rumors circulated that the Commissioners were going to purchase the land for Gage Park and make it the western linchpin of their new recreational system. This precipitated a real estate boom in the district. The land for the park (which was located on the southwest corner of 55th Street and Western) and for Garfield Boulevard (which joins Washington Park and Gage Park) was not purchased until 1873, but land values had already skyrocketed, driven up by speculators eager to capitalize on the anticipated recreational grounds.

There was another reason for the upsurge in the price of Gage Park land in the 1870s. A rumor of a projected railroad along Central Park Avenue focused attention on the western half of the present neighborhood. By 1880, the Chicago and Grand Trunk Railway (later the Grand Trunk Western, and now part of the Canadian National system) entered the city via this route. This railroad was especially important in the economic history of the city, for during the 1870s and 1880s, it was the only line willing to haul the refrigerated railroad cars that were developed by Gustavus Swift and other Chicago packers. One result of the construction of the Grand Trunk was the establishment of the settlement of Elsdon near 51st and Kedzie. In 1885 the population of the thirty frame cottages which made up this hamlet was mostly German, though there were a few Irish families there as well. Truck farming was still the chief activity in the area.

Gage Park was annexed to Chicago in 1889. A year later the Archdiocese of Chicago established a parish church for the residents of Elsdon and the surrounding farmers. The parish of St. Gall was founded by Father James A. Hemlock as a mission of St. Agnes's parish in Brighton Park. The

parish retained its missionary status for nine years, with mass being celebrated in a rented building at 52nd Street and Turner for twenty-one years. In 1916 the present site of the parish church at 55th and Kedzie was purchased and a building was erected there with volunteer labor supplied by the parishioners. Four years later the membership of St. Gall's included sixteen nationalities, a reflection of the diversity of population which has been characteristic of Gage Park. This neighborhood has never been dominated by any single ethnic group.

Growth was slow in Gage Park through the 1890s. Then, in 1902, electric street railway lines were pushed south along Western Avenue and Kedzie, connecting the community area with the city. From 1905, when there were 575 residential structures, to 1919, the neighborhood experienced a housing boom along its still unpaved streets. As in Brighton Park and other neighborhoods located south and west of the stockyard district, this population increase was the result of the exodus of upwardly mobile workers from the Back of the Yards, especially from the noisy and dirty section immediately adjacent to the packinghouses. By 1920 Gage Park had

13,692 inhabitants. One-third of these were foreign born, compared with Back of the Yards which showed 50 percent foreign born in the same census. The Polish and the Czechoslovakians predominated in the area, while Germans already had begun to move farther south across 59th Street.

During the growth boom between 1905 and 1919, another Catholic church, the parish of St. Clare of Montefalco, was established in Gage Park. St. Clare began as a mission of St. Rita of Cascia, the latter founded in 1905 in the Chicago Lawn neighborhood just south of Gage Park. Like St. Gall's, St. Clare's had a mixed ethnic congregation composed of Poles, Germans, Irish, Czechs, Slovaks, and Yugoslavs. The Archdiocese conferred separate status on it in 1916.

During the first three decades of the twentieth century, Gage Park and the areas adjacent to it experienced increased industrial development resulting from progress in the construction and connecting of Chicago's beltline railroads. The Kenwood Manufacturing District, which lies partly in Brighton Park and partly in Gage Park, was opened during this period, as was the Clearing Industrial District, located southwest of the community. Other industries were established along Western Avenue. The latter industrial development was an outgrowth of the Central Manufacturing District originally sited in the stockyards district.

The industrial movement along Western Avenue and its continuation, Western Boulevard, indicates the varied character of this thoroughfare. The avenue was laid out as part of Blue Island Plank Road by the developer of Brighton Park. The portion known as Western Boulevard was planned two decades later by the South Park Commission as part of its comprehensive park and boulevard system for the South Side. But instead of becoming the wide and beautiful boulevard envisioned by the South Park Commission or the center of business and commerce hoped for by the founders of Brighton Park, Western Avenue (Boulevard) sports commercial establishments, light and heavy manufacturing concerns, and residents. The thoroughfare functions as a major crosstown travel corridor and the steady flow of traffic along its course is its chief characteristic.

Western Avenue's auto- and truck-carrying capacity was an important factor in the further development of Gage Park. During the 1920s the population of the neighborhood more than doubled, reaching 31,535 by 1930. In the course of that growth decade, Gage Park assumed its present residential character: builders erected inexpensive brick bungalows and two-flats that catered to the upwardly mobile working class as did similar developments in neighboring Brighton Park. In 1940, 67.7 percent of the 7,824 residential units in Gage Park were single-family dwellings, and 57.7 percent of the total units were owner-occupied. In the same year the New City community area, in which the Back of the Yards is located, could claim only 21.7 percent of 10,055 units as single-family dwellings and only 31.9 percent of all units as owner-occupied.

As the Great Depression and then World War II engulfed the nation, Gage Park still had a number of open lots on which the first house had not yet been erected. After the war, however, these lots soon filled up with single- and multi-family dwellings. Between 1940 and 1970, 1,544 units of housing were constructed in Gage Park, quite a high percentage compared to the situation in other community areas farther north which had been built up earlier. Each decade witnessed less construction, however, and between 1960 and 1970, only 109 new units were added to the housing stock in Gage Park.

This seeming continuity conceals one significant housing change that has occurred since 1960. In that year 62.1 percent of all units were owner-occupied. A decade later this number had slipped to 52.4 percent. These statistics reflect the fact that the new buildings were largely apartment houses. These multiple-unit dwellings are located mainly in the western third of the community and cater to young couples just getting started or to those with only one or two small children. The population in the eastern two-thirds of the neighborhood, meanwhile, has grown older. In 1950, only 6.2 percent of the 31,535 inhabitants were 65 or older, compared with twenty years later when 14.9 of the 26,698 residents were in that category. Of all the neighborhoods covered in this volume, Gage Park has the highest percentage of those 65 and over. Given this age composition and the fact that the areas directly to the east—notably Englewood, West Englewood, and the fringes of the Back of the Yards—have experienced a dramatic increase in black population since 1960, it would appear that this community area is susceptible to rapid racial change if it follows the neighborhood succession process of other areas closer to the city center.

Today Gage Park remains a lower middle-class and working-class neighborhood. While rents and mean values of single-family dwellings are higher than in Brighton Park or Back of the Yards, they are lower than those for the city as a whole. In 1970 the mean rent in the area was $101, or 12 percent lower than that for the citywide

Becvar Funeral Home, 5220 S. Kedzie Avenue, 1955. This establishment was founded by a Bohemian, Frank Becvar, in 1907 at 47th and Lincoln (now Wolcott). His sons took it over after it was moved to its present location in 1922. Cousins James and George Becvar, grandsons of the founder, are the current owners. Photo by Arthur M. Weiland, CHS.

The Elsdon Station of the Chicago, Grand Trunk, and Western Railroad, 3601 W. 51st Street, 1962. Originally a suburban commuter station, the building had been converted into a freight and switchyard office by the time this photograph was taken. Photo by Tom H. Long, CHS.

measure, while the mean value of owner-occupied units was $18,754, or nearly $4,000 less than for all of Chicago.

Income figures and job listings further reinforce the impression that Gage Park is lower middle class and working class in character. Some 71.9 percent of the area families made below $15,000 in 1970. Of all those residents who were working, 83.7 percent of the males and 89.0 percent of the females were employed by private industry, while 8.2 percent and 5.9 percent, respectively, of these categories worked for local government. This latter figure is important politically, for it helps explain the community's attachment to the Democratic Party organization.

The 1970 census figures indicated that the nuclear family remains strong in this community. Of all children under 18 years of age, 88.3 percent lived with both parents.

Like other communities on Chicago's Southwest Side, Gage Park made national news headlines in the 1960s. The open housing marches led by Dr. Martin Luther King, Jr., were met with open hostility by Gage Parkers. During these encounters, many neighborhood residents stated publicly that they had left other communities to the east rather than live with blacks. Much of the racial controversy that continues is over the quality of education in Gage Park High School, which is located at the west end of the 27-acre park from which the community derives its name. Today, many of the students who attend Gage Park High are blacks from the neighborhoods east of the park and whites from the area to the west.

On several occasions there have been clashes among the students. These incidents were not inevitable, but the likelihood of their reoccurrence has increased because of a particular population movement toward Gage Park. While the United States Census does not include a count of second, third, or fourth generation ethnics, church records indicate that the ethnic identity of one group in Gage Park has been reinforced in the past two decades through the arrival of newcomers of Irish extraction.

The route of this Irish inflow has been west on Garfield Boulevard. Parish histories provide a means for tracing this movement. In the early 1860s a group of Irish Catholics began to meet at the home of a Mr. Fagin on South State Street, and in 1865 the Chicago Archdiocese recognized the existence of the congregation by authorizing the mission of St. Anne. The parish of St. Anne (now the parish of St. Charles Lwanga) was founded in 1869 on the corner of Garfield Boulevard and Wentworth Avenue (200 west). A second Irish church was the parish of the Visitation founded in 1886. Its first services were held at the Sherman Public School at 51st and Morgan (1000 west). The congregation then erected a church on 53rd and Morgan and moved to its present building on Garfield at Peoria (900 west) in 1896. An elementary school and a girl's high school were also established by the Visitation congregation.

The next westward movement of the Irish along Garfield involved St. Basil's. The first building to house this congregation was an old blacksmith shop at 53rd and Ashland (1600 west). The present St. Basil's church was opened at Garfield and Wood (1800 west) in 1904. Through the twentieth century the Irish continued westward along Garfield, with new members joining the parish of St. Gall's and St. Clare of Montefalco in Gage Park.

During the last two decades, Visitation parish has lost practically all of its Irish congregants and St. Basil's appears to be facing the same prospect. The movement of blacks along Garfield has led many former members of these congregations to move to Gage Park.

The future of Gage Park is difficult to ascertain principally because so many complex forces are at work there. Many of the neighborhood's residents already have moved west from Englewood, West Englewood, and Back of the Yards. The tightness of the present housing market may create a more stable situation than has been evident since World War II. The continuing decentralization of employment and increased use of the auto, however, may offset these conditions. Yet another possibility is that young couples will find Gage Park's relatively low-priced housing sufficiently attractive to settle there, bringing new resources to this Southwest Side neighborhood.

In sum, many of the forces that have brought major change to other South Side communities now are at work in Gage Park. The outcome may well be an important indicator of what will happen to other similar neighborhoods throughout the city of Chicago.

St. Simon Catholic Church, 5157 S. California Avenue, 1966. Organized in 1926 when a group of Slovak families broke away from St. Michael the Archangel, the congregation met in temporary quarters until this building was erected in 1928. A former altar boy at St. Simon, John Petrik, is now the pastor of the church. Photo by Casey Prunchunas, CHS.

Sawyer Public School, 5248 S. Sawyer Avenue, 1955. The original eight rooms of this school were built in 1901. Another sixteen were added in 1917. Photo by Arthur Weiland, CHS.

Saint Peter and Paul Carpatho-Russian Greek Orthodox Catholic Church, 5244 S. Western Avenue, 1966. The congregation comprised only 70 families when this church, built "to resemble the Byzantine churches of ancient Greece and Russia," was erected in 1931. The onion dome on its steeple is a symbol of the Orthodox faith. The parish celebrated its fiftieth anniversary the year this photograph was taken; it then numbered more than 700 families. Photo by Casey Prunchunas, CHS.

2600 block of W. 51st Street, 1955. The addition of stone facing and a new entrance were part of the extensive remodeling done by the Economy Savings and Loan Association in the early 1950s. The other buildings date from the 1910s and 1920s, when Gage Park experienced its most rapid growth. Photo by Arthur M. Weiland, CHS.

EPILOGUE

It has never been easy to maintain a neighborhood. After all, community areas are only small pieces of the city and have been beset by the same forces of change that have affected Chicago and, indeed, all large cities. The major result of these changes has been continued decentralization. For old neighborhoods like those on Chicago's South Side, that national movement has translated into exodus: few of the fifteen residential neighborhoods examined in this volume have as large a population now as they had a decade or so ago.

One local consequence of these changes is that many South Siders have come to regard their neighborhoods in much the same light as suburbanites do theirs: a place to live in, although their work, social, and recreational activities and familial connections may extend over a much larger radius. Almost universal access to automobiles and telephones has made this kind of living and the manifold choices it implies possible.

Viewed in this context, the progressive closing of the stockyards and Packingtown during the past three decades takes on more importance. Not only were these facilities the area's chief employer, they were also its most enduring symbol. For many families the closing of the stockyards removed the economic incentive to live on the South Side, and those who remain now commute to work, as do the predominantly black residents of Oakland, Douglas, Grand Boulevard, and Washington Park.

The University of Chicago, Michael Reese Hospital, Mercy Hospital, and the Illinois Institute of Technology perform for their respective communities some of the same functions that Packingtown and the stockyards did for their neighborhoods, but with a difference. The stockyards were the reason for the development of the surrounding neighborhoods and continued to infuse them with economic vitality. These medical and educational institutions, however, did not originally provide the impetus for the development of their surrounding communities but have now become anchors for their revitalization.

The changes described in this account have left an ambiguous legacy on which to maintain community life. Where they have been strong and cohesive, community organizations have helped preserve neighborhood ties and rebuild old institutions. But in the process they have used up enormous resources. Unless the residents of these areas can continue to find new capital from the private sector and obtain more financial backing from public sources, the demolition ball may again swing into rapid motion to raze neighborhoods long peopled with diverse populations.

No wholly satisfactory method by which old neighborhoods can renew themselves has as yet been devised. The histories in this volume recount half a century of effort by South Siders to deal with this problem. Saving old neighborhoods or building new ones has become a matter of concern not only for community residents but also for local, regional, and national policymakers. If the neighborhood way of life is valued sufficiently to draw a strong and continuing commitment of organizational and financial resources then the neighborhoods will have a chance to survive.

BIBLIOGRAPHY

General

Abbott, Edith. *The Tenements of Chicago, 1908–1935*. Chicago, 1936.

Andreas, Alfred T. *History of Chicago*. 3 vols. Chicago, 1884–86.

———. *History of Cook County, Illinois*. Chicago, 1884.

Bourne, Larry S., ed. *Internal Structure of the City. Readings on Space and Environment*. New York, 1971.

Bowly, Devereaux, Jr. *The Poorhouse: Subsidized Housing in Chicago, 1895–1976*. Carbondale and Edwardsville, Ill., 1978.

Chamberlain, Everett. *Chicago and Its Suburbs*. Chicago, 1874.

Chicago Area Transportation Study. *Final Report*. 3 vols. Chicago, 1959–62.

Chicago Association of Commerce and Industry Research and Statistics Division and OSLA Financial Services Corporation. *Community Area Data Book for the City of Chicago. 1970 Census Data by 75 Community Areas*. Chicago, n. d.

Chicago City Council Committee on Railway Terminals and Citizens Committee on River Straightening. *The Straightening of the Chicago River*. Chicago, 1926.

The Chicago Clubs. Illustrated. Chicago, 1888.

Chicago Plan Commission. *Chicago Land Use Survey. Housing in Chicago Communities. Prepared by the Works Projects Administration Under the Direction of the Chicago Plan Commission*. 75 vols. Chicago, 1940.

———. *Chicago Land Use Survey*. Vol. 1, *Residential Chicago*. Vol. 2, *Land Use in Chicago*, Chicago, 1942 and 1943.

———. *Forty-Four Cities in the City of Chicago*. Chicago, 1942.

Chicago Transit Authority Engineer's Office. *Chronological Order of Service Changes*. Rev. mimeographed. Chicago, 1961.

———. *Historical Information, 1859–1965*. Mimeographed. Chicago, 1966.

Drury, John. *Old Chicago Houses*. Chicago, 1941.

Duncan, Beverly, and Hauser, Philip M. *Housing a Metropolis—Chicago*. Glencoe, Ill., 1960.

Flinn, John T. *History of the Chicago Police*. Chicago, 1887.

Greeley, Andrew M. *The Communal Catholic*. New York, 1976.

Hauser, Philip M., and Kitagawa, Evelyn M. *Local Community Fact Book for Chicago, 1950*. Chicago, 1953.

Hoyt, Homer. *One Hundred Years of Land Values in Chicago, 1830–1933*. Chicago, 1933.

———. *The Structure and Growth of Residential Neighborhoods in American Cities*. Washington, D.C., 1939.

Hunter, Robert. *Tenement Conditions in Chicago*. Chicago, 1901.

Journal, Town of Lake, [Chicago]. *Golden Jubilee Edition*. September 14, 1939.

Keller, Suzanne. *The Urban Neighborhood: A Sociological Perspective*. New York, 1968.

Kitagawa, Evelyn M., and Taeuber, Karl E., eds. *Local Community Fact Book, Chicago Metropolitan Area, 1960*. Chicago, 1963.

Landmarks Preservation Council and Service. *Chicago's Landmark Structures: An Inventory. Central Area*. Chicago, 1975.

Lind, Alan R. *Chicago Surface Lines: An Illustrated History*. Park Forest, Ill., 1974.

Mayer, Harold M. *The Railway Pattern of Metropolitan Chicago*. Chicago, 1943.

Mayer, Harold M., and Wade, Richard C. *Chicago, Growth of a Metropolis*. Chicago, 1969.

Meyerson, Martin, and Banfield, Edward C. *Politics, Planning, and the Public Interest*. Glencoe, Ill., 1955.

Mimar, D. W., and Greer, Scott. *The Concept of Community: Readings with Interpretations*. Chicago, 1969.

"Our Suburbs." *Chicago Times*, October 10, 1869.

Out of Town, Being a Distinctive Historical and Statistical Account of the Suburban Towns and Residences of Chicago. Chicago, 1869.

Palmer, Vivien M. *Social Backgrounds of Chicago's Local Communities*. Chicago, 1930.

The Parks and Property Interests of the City of Chicago. Chicago, 1869.

Pierce, Bessie Louise. *A History of Chicago*. 3 vols. New York, 1937–57.

Proudfoot, Malcolm J. "The Major Outlying Business Districts of Chicago." Ph.D. dissertation, University of Chicago, 1936.

Quaife, Milo M. *Chicago's Highways Old and New: From Indian Trails to Motor Road*. Chicago, 1923.

Reckless, Walter C. *Vice in Chicago*. Chicago, 1933.

Suttles, Gerald D. *The Social Order of the Slum*. Chicago, 1969.

The University of Chicago Center for Urban Studies. *Mid-Chicago Economic Development Study*. 3 vols. Chicago, 1966.

The University of Chicago Community Inventory. *Guide for Coding Street Address to Community Area and Census Tract, Chicago, 1960*. Chicago, 1961.

The University of Chicago Local Community Research Committee. *History of Communit[ies], Chicago.* Prepared for the Chicago Historical Society and the Local Community Research Committee, University of Chicago. Research under the direction of Vivien M. Palmer. Typescript. 6 vols. Chicago, 1925–30.

Ward, David. *Cities and Immigrants: A Geography of Change in Nineteenth Century America.* New York, 1971.

Welfare Council of Metropolitan Chicago. *1970 Census Data. Report Number Two. General Population and Housing Characteristics. Chicago Community Areas.* Chicago, 1971.

Welfare Council of Metropolitan Chicago Research Department. *Chicago Community Area Profiles.* Chicago, 1964.

Wirth, Louis. *The Ghetto.* Chicago, 1928.

Wirth, Louis, and Bernert, Eleanor H., eds. *Local Community Fact Book of Chicago.* Chicago, 1949.

Wirth, Louis, and Furez, Margaret, eds. *Local Community Fact Book, 1938.* Chicago, 1938.

Atlases and Directories

The Chicago Blue Book of Selected Names of Chicago and Suburban Towns. Chicago, 1892–1916.

Chicago Telephone Directories. 1899–1978. (Title varies.)

The Elite Directory and Club List of Chicago. . . . Chicago, 1886–90.

Greeley [Samuel S.] & [Gustaf H.] Carlson's Atlas of the Village of Hyde Park. Vol. 1. Chicago, 1880 (updated to 1888).

Greeley, Carlson & Company. *Atlas of the Town of Lake.* Vol. 1. Chicago, 1883.

Hall & Co's Chicago City Directory and Business Advertizer for 1854–55. Chicago, 1855. (Directory titles and publishers vary through 1929.)

Rascher Insurance Map Publishing Company. *Rascher's Atlas of Chicago.* Vol. 8, 1887 (updated to 1891); Vol. 11, 1885 (updated to 1891); Vol. 13, 1890–91. Chicago, 1885–91.

_____. *Rascher's Atlas of the North Half of Hyde Park.* Chicago, 1890.

Reversed Directory of the Elite of Chicago. . . . Chicago, 1881–85.

Robinson's Atlas of the City of Chicago, Illinois. 5 vols. New York, 1886.

Sanborn Map Co. *Chicago.* [Map] Vol. 12, 1896 (updated to 1922); Vol. 14, 1895 (updated to 1925). Chicago, 1895–96.

Manuscript and Reference Collections

Chicago. Chicago Historical Society. Mary McDowell Papers.

Chicago. Chicago Historical Society Library. Newspaper clipping files, headings on specific neighborhoods, buildings, and people.

Chicago. Chicago Historical Society. University of Chicago Settlement House Papers.

Chicago. University of Chicago Library. Ernest W. Burgess Papers.

Ethnic, Racial, and Religious Groups

American Jewish Congress. *A Guide to Jewish Chicago.* Chicago, 1974.

Beijbom, Ulf. *Swedes in Chicago. A Demographic and Social Study of the 1846–1880 Immigration.* Stockholm, 1971.

Bullard, Thomas. "Distribution of Chicago's Germans, 1850–1914." Master's thesis, University of Chicago, 1969.

Chicago Community Renewal Program Study. *An Atlas of Chicago's People, Jobs and Homes.* Chicago, 1963.

Chicago Department of Development and Planning. *Historic City: The Settlement of Chicago.* Chicago, 1976.

_____. *The People of Chicago: Who We Are and Who We Have Been. Census Data on Foreign Stock and Race, 1837–1970 [with] Mother Tongue Addendum, 1910–1970.* Chicago, 1976.

Cressy, Paul Frederick. "The Succession of Cultural Groups in the City of Chicago." Ph.D. dissertation, University of Chicago, 1930.

Drake, St. Clair, and Cayton, Horace. *Black Metropolis: A Study of Negro Life in a Northern City.* New York, 1945.

Duncan, Otis Dudley, and Duncan, Beverly. *The Negro Population of Chicago. A Study of Residential Succession.* Chicago, 1957.

Evans, Rev. John, comp. *Chicagoland Directory of Religion, 1950.* Chicago, 1950.

Fang, John T. C. *Chinatown: Handy Guide.* Chicago, 1959.

Garraghan, Gilbert J. *Catholic Church in Chicago, 1673–1871.* Chicago, 1921.

Greene, Victor. *For God and Country: The Rise of Polish and Lithuanian Ethnic Consciousness in America, 1860–1910.* Madison, Wisc., 1975.

Gutstein, Morris Aaron. *A Priceless Heritage: The Epic Growth of Nineteenth Century Chicago Jewry.* New York, 1953.

Habig, Marion A. *The Franciscans at St. Augustine's and in Chicagoland.* Chicago, 1961.

Hofmeister, Rudolph A. *The Germans in Chicago.* Urbana, Ill., 1976.

Horak, Jakub. "Assimilation of Czechs in Chicago." Ph. D. dissertation, University of Chicago, 1920.

Illustrated Souvenir of the Archdiocese of Chicago. Chicago, 1916.

Kantowitz, Edward R. *Polish-American Politics in Chicago.* Chicago, 1975.

Meites, Hyman L., ed. *History of the Jews of Chicago,* Chicago, 1924.

Nelli, Humbert S. *The Italians in Chicago, 1880–1930. A Study in Ethnic Mobility.* New York, 1970.

Parot, Joseph John. "The American Faith and the Persistence of Chicago Polonia, 1870–1920." Ph.D. dissertation, Northern Illinois University, 1971.

Phillips, George S. [Janway Searle]. *Chicago and Her Churches.* Chicago, 1868.

Piper, Ruth M. "The Irish in Chicago, 1848–1871." Master's thesis, University of Chicago, 1936.

Poles of Chicago, 1837–1937; A History of One Century of Polish Contribution to the City of Chicago, Illinois. Chicago, 1937.

Schafer, Marvin Revel. "The Catholic Church in Chicago, Its Growth and Administration." Ph.D. dissertation, University of Chicago, 1929.

Schwartzkopf, Louis J. *The Lutheran Trail.* St. Louis, 1950.

Souvenir of the Silver Jubilee in the Episcopacy of His Grace, the Most Reverend Patrick Augustine Feehan, Archbishop of Chicago, November 1, 1890. Chicago, 1891.

Spear, Allan. *Black Chicago: The Making of a Negro Ghetto, 1890–1920.* Chicago, 1967.

Stackhouse, Perry J. *Chicago and the Baptists: A Century of Progress.* Chicago, 1933.

Taeuber, Karl, and Taeuber, Alma. *Negroes in Cities.* Chicago, 1965.

Thompson, Joseph J. *The Archdiocese of Chicago, Antecedents and Development.* Des Plaines, Ill., 1920.

Townsend, Andrew Jacke. *The Germans of Chicago.* Chicago, 1932.

Wilson, Margaret Gibbons. "Concentrations and Dispersal of the Chinese Population of Chicago, 1870 to the Present." Master's thesis, University of Chicago, 1969.

Loop

Banham, Reyner. "A Walk in the Loop." *Chicago* 2 (1965): 25–27.

Breese, Gerald William. *The Daytime Population of the Central Business District, With Particular*

Reference to the Factor of Transportation. Chicago, 1969.

Chicago Central Area Committee. *The Chicago Central Area—Today; A Six Year Report.* Chicago, 1962.

_____. *Chicago 21, A Plan for the Central Area Communities.* Chicago, 1973.

Chicago Department of City Planning. *Development Plan for the Central Area of Chicago.* . . . Chicago, 1958.

Condit, Carl. *The Rise of the Skyscraper.* Chicago, 1952.

_____. *Chicago: Building, Planning, and Urban Technology.* Vol. 1, *1910–1929.* Vol. 2, *1930–1970.* Chicago, 1973, 1974.

Johnson, Earl Shepard. "The Natural History of the Central Business District with Particular Reference to Chicago." Ph.D. dissertation, University of Chicago, 1941.

Landmarks Preservation Council and Service. *Chicago's Landmark Structures: An Inventory. Loop Area.* Chicago, 1974.

Randall, Frank A. *History of the Development of Building Construction in Chicago.* Urbana, Ill., 1949.

Stock Yards/CMD

Abbott, Edith, and Breckenridge, Sophonisba P. "Women in Industry, the Chicago Stockyards." *Journal of Political Economy* 19 (October 1911): 632–54.

Brody, David. *The Butcher Workmen.* Cambridge, Mass., 1964.

Central Manufacturing District. *Speaking of Ourselves.* Chicago, ca. 1942.

"The Central Manufacturing District Through the Eyes of Others." *CMD Magazine* 25 (1941): 97–134.

Fowler, Bertram Baynes. *Men, Meat and Miracles.* New York, 1952.

Grand, W. Joseph. *Illustrated History of the Union Stock Yards.* Chicago, 1896.

Hill, Howard C. "The Development of Chicago as a Center of the Meat Packing Industry." *Mississippi Valley Historical Review* 3 (December 1923): 253–73.

Meyers, Howard Barton. "The Policing of Labor Disputes in Chicago: A Case Study." Ph.D. dissertation, University of Chicago, 1929.

1953 Yearbook of Figures of the Livestock Trade. Chicago, 1953.

Parkhurst, William. *History of the Yards, 1865–1953.* Chicago, 1953.

Schoop, Mary D. "50 Golden Years." Series in *CMD Magazine* 39 (June-October 1955).

Schryrer, Clyde H. "Record of Achievement Written by District." *CMD Magazine* 11 (1927): 16.

Swift, Louis Franklin. *The Yankee of the Yards.* Chicago, 1927.

Wade, Louise Carroll. "Burnham & Root's Stockyards Connection." *Chicago History* 4 (Fall 1975): 139–47.

Wentworth, Edna Louise Clark. "The History of the Controversy between Labor and Capital in the Slaughtering and Meat Packing Industries of Chicago." Master's thesis, University of Chicago, 1922.

Winans, Charles. *The Evolution of a Vast Industry.* Chicago, 1935.

Wing, Jack. *The Great Union Stock Yards of Chicago.* Chicago, 1865.

Near South Side

Chicago Land Clearance Commission. *Michael Reese–Prairie Shores Redevelopment Project. Final Project Report.* Chicago, 1962.

Drury, John. "Old Chicago Neighborhoods. XII. Near South Side." *Landlord's Guide* 39 (March 1948): 12–15.

Dyer, Victor. *Prairie Avenue: An Annotated Bibliography.* Chicago, 1977.

Freeman, Lucy. *Hospital in Action: The Story of Michael Reese Medical Center.* New York, 1956.

"Lake Meadows: A Suburb Within a City." *Ebony* 16 (1960): 27–35.

Ledermann, Robert Charles. "Industrial Functions in Chicago's Near South Area." Master's thesis, University of Chicago, 1951.

McCahill, Ed. "South Loop: Building for the Future." *Chicago* 26 (December 1977): 154–61.

Michael Reese Hospital. *Regarding Reese: 75 Years of Progress, 1881–1956.* Chicago, 1956.

Priddy, Gladys. "Near South Side." *Chicago Tribune,* March 4, 1954.

Pruter, Robert. "The Prairie Avenue Section of Chicago: The History and Examination of Its Decline." Master's thesis, Roosevelt University, 1976.

South Side Planning Board. *An Opportunity to Rebuild Chicago through Industrial Development on the Central South Side.* Chicago, 1953.

Douglas

Chicago Housing Authority. *The Slum . . . Is Rehabilitation Possible?* Chicago, 1946.

Chicago Plan Commission. *Introducing the Central South Area Plan.* Chicago, 1960.

First Baptist Church of Chicago. *A Century and a Quarter with the First Baptist Church of Chicago.* Chicago, 1958.

Fisher, Miles Mark. "History of Olivet Baptist Church of Chicago." Master's thesis, University of Chicago, 1922.

Hendricks, Walter. "Historical Sketch of Armour Institute of Technology." *American Engineer and Alumnus* 2 (1937): 34–40.

Illinois Institute of Technology. *Technology Center Today and Tomorrow. A Building and Expansion Program.* . . . Chicago, 1949 (?).

Mississippi Vista. *The Brothers of the Christian Schools in the Mid-West, 1849–1949.* Winona, Minn., 1948.

Peebles, James Clinton. *A History of Armour Institute of Technology.* . . . Chicago, 1955 (?).

Oakland

Drury, John. "Old Chicago Neighborhoods. XXIX. Oakland." *Landlord's Guide* 41 (April 1950): 10–11.

Kenwood-Ellis Community Center. *Community Handbook.* . . . Chicago, 1956.

_____. *Community Facts.* . . . Chicago, 1956.

"The Oakland District." *The Graphic* 12 (March 22, 1890): supp. 1–4.

Oakland-Kenwood Planning Association. *A Report to the Oakland-Kenwood Community.* . . . Chicago, 1952.

Kenwood

Drury, John. "Old Chicago Neighborhoods. IX. Kenwood." *Landlord's Guide* 38 (December 1947): 12.

Felsenthal, Bernard, and Eliassof, Herman. *History of Kehillath Anshe Maarabh (Congregation of the Men of the West).* . . . Chicago, 1897.

Kenwood Town Homes Company. *A Position Paper on the Redevelopment Controversy in Kenwood.* Chicago, ca. 1964.

Kenwood-Ellis Community Center. *Community Facts.* . . . Chicago, 1956.

Picturesque Kenwood, Hyde Park, Illinois: Its Artistic Homes, Boulevards, Drives, Scenery and Surroundings. . . . Chicago, ca. 1886.

Richey, Elinor. "Kenwood Foils the Block-busters." *Harper's Magazine* 227 (August 1963): 42–47.

"Your Neighborhood Kenwood." *Chicago Sunday Times,* December 24, 1939.

Hyde Park

Abrahamson, Julia. *A Neighborhood Finds Itself.* New York, 1959.

Ayer, Janet [Hopkins]. "Old Hyde Park." In *Chicago Yesterdays: A Sheaf of Reminiscences,* edited by Caroline Kirkland. Chicago, 1919, 179–92.

Beadle, Muriel. *The Hyde Park-Kenwood Urban Renewal Years. A History to Date.* Chicago, 1964.

Block, Jean F. *Hyde Park Houses: An Informal History, 1856–1910.* Chicago, 1978.

Callahan, Tom. "Chicago Starts to Revive Old Respected Neighborhood. . . ." *Commerce* 52 (February 1955): 18.

Chicago. Chicago Historical Society. *Hyde Park* by Lucretia S. Harper. Typescript. 3 vols.

Drury, John. "Old Chicago Neighborhoods. I. Proud Hyde Park. . . ." *Landlord's Guide* 38 (April 1947): 4–8. ·

Goodspeed, Thomas Wakefield. *The Story of the University of Chicago, 1890–1925.* Chicago, 1925.

Hyde Park Herald. "An Anniversary Edition Celebrating Our 75th Year of Publication. . . . October 3, 1956."

Hyde Park-Kenwood Community Conference. *This is Hyde Park-Kenwood: Past, Present, Future.* Chicago, 1959.

Hyde Park Now and Then. Published to Commemorate the Opening of the Hyde Park-Kenwood National Bank Building, April 20, 1929. Chicago, 1929.

"Hyde Park: Study in Urban Renewal." *Illinois Central Magazine* 51 (August 1959): 10–11.

Levi, Julian. *The Neighborhood Program of the University of Chicago.* Chicago, 1961 (?).

McGiffert, Arthur Cushman, Jr. *No Ivory Tower: The Story of the Chicago Theological Seminary.* Chicago, 1965.

Matsoukas, Nick John, and Hyman Sidney, eds. *Portrait of Hyde Park.* Chicago, 1939.

Peirce, Daniel A. "Old Days in Hyde Park." [Chicago] *South Side Review,* March 30, 1923.

Perloff, Harvey. *Urban Renewal in a Chicago Neighborhood: An Appraisal of the Hyde Park-Kenwood Renewal Program.* Chicago, 1955.

Press, Valetta. *Hyde Park/Kenwood. A Case Study of Urban Renewal. . . .* Chicago, 1971.

Rossi, Peter H., and Dentler, Robert A. *The Politics of Urban Renewal: The Chicago Findings.* Glencoe, Ill., 1961.

Storr, Richard J. *Harper's University: The Beginnings; A History of the University of Chicago.* Chicago, 1966.

University of Chicago. *Saving Our Cities. The University of Chicago Pioneers Urban Renewal in Own Neighborhood.* Chicago, 1955 (?).

University of Chicago Program of Education and Research in Planning. *The University of Chicago and the Surrounding Community. The University's Role in Community Conservation and Improvement.* Chicago, 1953.

"University Real Estate Holdings in the Campus Area as of June 30, 1976." *The University of Chicago Record* 5 (November 5, 1976): 164–67.

Willard, Laura. "Local Government in Illinois as Illustrated by the Municipal Development of Hyde Park." Master's thesis, University of Chicago, 1895.

"Your Neighborhood Hyde Park." *Chicago Sunday Times,* July 16, 1939.

Grand Boulevard

Provident Hospital and Training School. *Fifty Years with Provident Hospital, 1891–1941. A Statement to Alumni and Friends Regarding the Golden Jubilee Celebration.* Chicago, 1941.

Sisters of Mercy. Saint Xavier's Chicago. *Reminiscences of Seventy Years, 1846–1916.* Chicago, 1916.

Washington Park

Duis, Perry R., and Holt, Glen E. "Chicago As It Was: Bright Lights, Hard Times of White City II." *Chicago* 27 (August 1978): 176–79.

_____. "Chicago As It Was: Derby Day at Washington Park." *Chicago* 27 (December 1978): 266–70.

Back of the Yards

Auksinis Jubiliejus, 1892–1942. Sv. Jurgio Parapija. (Golden Jubilee, 1892–1942, St. George's Parish). Chicago, 1942.

Breckinridge, Sophonisba P., and Abbott, Edith. "Housing Conditions in Chicago, Ill. The Twenty-Ninth Ward Back of the Yards." *The American Journal of Sociology* 16 (January 1911): 433–68.

Dedication of Church and School. St. Rose of Lima. Chicago, 1940.

Golden Jubilee of Holy Cross Lithuanian Roman Catholic Parish, 1909–1954. Chicago, 1954.

Program and Chronological History. Souvenir of St. Augustine's Parish Golden Jubilee, 1886–(1881)–1936. Chicago, 1936.

Sacred Heart of Jesus Parish Golden Jubilee Book, 1910–1960. Chicago, 1960.

St. John of God Parish Golden Jubilee Book, 1907–1957. Chicago, 1957.

Sinclair, Upton. *The Jungle.* Reprint. New York, 1947.

Skillin, Edward, Jr. "Back of the Stockyards." [Reprint from] *The Commonweal,* November 29, 1940.

"Your Neighborhood New City." *Chicago Sunday Times,* October 22, 1939.

Canaryville

Carey, E. F., M.D. "History of Canaryville." *Chicago Tribune,* June 25, 1949.

_____. "When Leprechauns Came to Chicago." *Chicago Tribune,* July 10, 1949.

Griffin, Richard T. "Big Jim O'Leary: 'Gambler Boss iv th' Yards'." *Chicago History* 5 (Winter 1976–77): 213–22.

United Charities of Chicago. *The Poverty of a Great City. 1914–15 Year Book of the United Charities of Chicago.* Chicago, 1915.

Bridgeport

Fanning, Charles F., Jr. "Mr. Dooley's Bridgeport Chronicle." *Chicago History* 2 (Spring 1972): 47–57.

Hughes, Elizabeth. "Chicago Housing Conditions. IX: The Lithuanians in the Fourth Ward." *The American Journal of Sociology* 20 (November 1914): 289–312.

Larsen, Carl W. "Your Neighborhood Bridgeport." *Chicago Sunday Times,* August 27, 1939.

Armour Square

All Saints–St. Anthony of Padua Parishes Centennial. Chicago, 1975.

Santa Lucia Silver Jubilee Book. Chicago, 1968.

Santa Maria Incoronata Church. *Golden Anniversary Book, 1904–1954.* Chicago, 1954.

McKinley Park

"History of McKinley Park is Colorful." *McKinley Park Life,* January 28, 1959.

"Your Neighborhood McKinley Park." *Chicago Sunday Times,* December 3, 1939.

Brighton Park

Hamzik, Joseph. "Gleanings of Archer Road." Typescript, 1961. Chicago Historical Society.

The Students of the Thomas Kelly High School. *The Kelly Community.* Chicago, 1938.

Gage Park

St. Bridget Church, 1850–1975. Chicago, 1975.

St. Gall Church Dedication, 1958. Chicago, 1958.

INDEX

All references are to page numbers. *Italicized* figures indicate captioned material; **boldface** figures indicate chapters dealing entirely with a specified neighborhood. Although street and railroad names appear frequently in this book, they have been indexed here only in those instances where substantive discussion occurs.

This book was set in Helvetica Light by
Publication Composition Corporation and
printed by Congress Printing Company, both
of Chicago, Illinois, U.S.A.